Praise for
Crossing the Street

"As investors work ever-more diligently to discover outsized returns in a complex global landscape, Andy Ho's book is a welcome and important contribution. His focus on Vietnam is distinctive and well-warranted. The book offers detailed, practical guidance for successful investing in this country, and its insights stem from extensive experience. Further, while the author has clearly had success as an investor, some of the book's lessons and insights are hard-won and so read not only as good and cautionary advice, but also offer compelling reading. Valuable for investors, those interested in the entrepreneurial landscape of Vietnam, and for those interested in economic development in the wider region."

David C. Schmittlein, PhD, Dean and Professor of Marketing at the MIT Sloan School of Management

"Telling Vietnam's story is critical to understanding the potential investment opportunities there, and Andy (along with his partner Don Lam) is superb at that. At the same time, he promotes patience and investment discipline as exemplified by the tips and learnings found in this book. Andy imparts universally important investment philosophies yet brings to bear his unique experiences in Vietnam. The frontier aspect of the country (although hopefully not for long), the juggling of international investors' desire for returns, liquidity and discount management and the unique political environment all have been managed well, and this book provides for a wonderful read."

Martin Glynn, VOF Director (2008–2014); Director, Sun Life Assurance Company of Canada; Chairman, Public Sector Pension Investment Board (PSP), Canada; Former President and CEO, HSBC Bank USA

"Andy Ho has accurately encapsulated the essence of investing in Vietnam. How, you may well ask, is it possible to equate a communist political regime with a dynamic and thriving business culture?

The answer inevitably has much to do with the dynamism and entrepreneurial spirit of the Vietnamese themselves, but also the extraordinary diaspora of Vietnamese connections across several continents that occurred after 1975. Andy Ho is himself a product of that diaspora who, like many others, returned to his native country.

I had the good fortune to get to know Andy well and to participate at an early stage in the growth of the Vietnamese economy. These many years later, I continue to hold shares in the fund and remain optimistic about Vietnam's prospects."

William Vanderfelt, VOF Chairman and
Director (2004–2013)

CROSSING
THE STREET

Every owner of a physical copy of this edition of

CROSSING THE STREET

can download the eBook for free direct from us at
Harriman House, in a DRM-free format that can be read
on any eReader, tablet or smartphone.

Simply head to:

ebooks.harriman-house.com/crossingthestreet

to get your copy now.

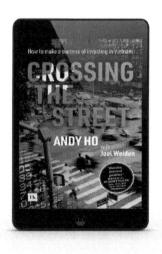

CROSSING THE STREET

HOW TO MAKE A SUCCESS OF INVESTING IN VIETNAM

ANDY HO

with Joel Weiden

Harriman House

HARRIMAN HOUSE LTD
3 Viceroy Court
Bedford Road
Petersfield
Hampshire
GU32 3LJ
GREAT BRITAIN
Tel: +44 (0)1730 233870

Email: enquiries@harriman-house.com
Website: harriman.house

First published in Great Britain in 2021.
Copyright © Andy Ho

Paperback ISBN: 978-0-85719-945-4
eBook ISBN: 978-0-85719-946-1

British Library Cataloguing in Publication Data
A CIP catalogue record for this book can be obtained from the British Library.

CONTENTS

PREFACE

It was late 2018 when I was first approached to write a book about my experiences investing in Vietnam. The previous year saw Vietnam's VN Index rank as the top-performing stock market in the world. Up 48% for the year, it was the talk of the investment industry. The first quarter of 2018 was also very good, with some IPOs and equitisations (or privatisations) of state-owned enterprises (SOEs). The market rose another 19%, again leading global indices. But this exuberance did not last – by the end of 2018, the VN Index had declined by 10%.

After a volatile year, 2019 ended on a better note, with the VN Index rising by over 7% (though some expected it to be twice that). There were no significant IPOs or equitisations to speak of during the year, but listed companies performed well. Going into 2020, expectations for the stock market were high, with many predicting a growth of 10–20%. But it was not meant to be. By the time I got to writing this book, Covid-19 was sweeping through the world and all bets were off.

All of this illustrates the unpredictability of the world we live in and of stock markets in particular – especially those in developing countries like Vietnam. Make no mistake though: Vietnam is the last significant opportunity for investors in Southeast Asia.

Since 2008, I have been fortunate enough to manage one of the largest Vietnam-focused funds. Listed on the London Stock Exchange, the fund I manage is called the VinaCapital Vietnam Opportunity Fund, or 'VOF' for short. Over the course of 12 years, Vietnam's stock market and economy have experienced numerous ups and downs. Indeed, there's a long-running joke that Vietnam always seems to be the 'next big thing'. Yet the country has never quite been able to reach its potential – at least not in the eyes of the global investment community.

But the stock market is just one indicator of a country's potential. VOF is unique among the Vietnam-focused funds in that it takes a multi-asset investment approach, investing in publicly traded companies as well as through private equity. In fact, most of our listed equity holdings originally entered our portfolio as private-equity investments. These investments are much more interesting to us as investment managers; they give us the opportunity to play a real role in adding value to the enterprise and, in turn, deliver solid returns to our investors over the long term.

Of course, there are no guarantees in investing. Like any other investor, we have had our share of mistakes along the way. Thankfully, those rare mistakes have worked to teach us just as much as our successes, and have helped define and guide how we approach our business. The rules outlined in this book are drawn from our 20 years of experience investing in Vietnam, as well as from others who have also invested in the country.

Investing in Vietnam, just as investing in any frontier or emerging market, carries risks – and hopefully commensurate returns. The path to development and success is never straight or straightforward. In some ways, change here can happen at a glacial pace and in ways that might leave outsiders scratching their heads.

However, some of us have always had confidence that the country would, eventually, build some real traction. It's why I first returned to Vietnam in 1994, once the United States began normalising its relationship with the country 20 years after the end of the war.

In 1977, I left Vietnam as a young child with my family on a boat bound for Malaysia. Like hundreds of thousands of Vietnamese people in those turbulent post-war years – especially those of Chinese heritage – we were seeking a better life. Eventually we made our way to Bridgeport, Connecticut. I didn't speak English – nor did I speak Vietnamese, as we spoke Cantonese at home – but I quickly learned.

At that time, the economy in Connecticut was not optimal for refugee families, so my grandfather sought better opportunities by heading west. We eventually settled in Denver, Colorado. Not long after we moved there, my grandfather tragically passed away from a stroke, due in part to the high altitude.

I think most of my family appreciated the selection of Denver as a place to plant our roots; it definitely gave me an appreciation for the outdoors. Like any other teenager in Colorado, I learned how to ski and enjoy the outdoors. After graduating from high school, I earned my bachelor's degree from the University of Colorado and joined Ernst & Young (EY) as an auditor.

Although I started out in EY's Denver office, I was quickly transferred to the Hong Kong office before moving to the newly opened office in Ho Chi Minh City (HCMC). EY had just purchased a small accounting firm in Vietnam and needed a team on the ground to start the new operation. I was fortunate to join this team and started to look after clients such as Coca-Cola and BP. It was this opening of EY Vietnam that first brought me back to the country I had fled with my family less than two decades earlier.

For nearly two years, I simply spent time in Vietnam, amazed by the excitement and optimism around me. While people were still quite poor and rode bicycles to get around HCMC, it seemed as if everyone had the goal of working hard and saving up to buy a Honda Dream motorbike (which at the time cost about $2,000; to put that in context, university graduates working for some of the few multinationals operating in the country were earning the princely sum of $200–400 a month!).

The optimism of the Vietnamese people was visible everywhere you looked. It seemed as if everybody was running a business – nearly every house converted their ground floor into some kind of shop, restaurant or other business. Everyone was working and saving. Everything was a start-up. And things were being built everywhere: office towers, apartment buildings and houses, roads, drains, bridges.

Ho Chi Minh City was like a real-life version of the computer game SimCity, which was wildly popular in the 1990s. And just like in SimCity, the airport and power plants needed to be developed, as well as a tax system established. Vietnam was still pretty much closed off to the rest of the world, so everything that was happening was kind of like a chemistry experiment in a lab: isolated and with few external influences. It was a fascinating time to be there and to witness a country just beginning to open itself up to the outside world.

It was during that two-year stint that I was able to properly learn Vietnamese, since everyone around me spoke it. If I had not been able to learn, I would not be where I am today. Knowing the language has been critical to investing in Vietnam, especially in the private-equity space.

It was also during my initial assignment in Vietnam that I met Tina Nguyen, the young lady who would become my wife. In 1998, I returned to the US to eventually pursue an MBA at the Massachusetts Institute of Technology. A year earlier, Tina moved to Montreal to pursue her career at EY Canada. She joined me in Cambridge in 1999.

After graduating, Tina and I moved to Austin, Texas, where I joined Dell Ventures, the venture capital arm of Dell Computers. We would eventually do the thing you usually only see in the movies – drive to Las Vegas on 31 December 1999 and get married. We wanted to get married before any potential fallout from the much-hyped Y2K issue – as it turned out, there was next to none. Anyway, the wedding wasn't at a drive-through chapel, but at city hall. Elvis was not there either, but my grandmother was. The 45-minute wedding service cost us $75.

Dell Ventures was a transformative experience – it really shaped my thinking around entrepreneurship, investing and how small businesses get built. I got to thinking that a lot of it was related to making mistakes. The foundation for what would become my 20 rules was poured.

As interesting as my time at Dell Ventures was, I left in 2004 for an enormous opportunity to become director of investment with Prudential Vietnam's fund-management company. In the role, I managed the capital markets portfolio and Prudential's bank-investment strategy. The chance to work in Vietnam's investment space was too good to pass up.

Unlike many Viet Kieu (or overseas Vietnamese), my family were not concerned when I expressed a desire to live in Vietnam full-time with my wife and child. My father had already returned to the country to resume practising as a physician and teaching, and I had other relatives still in the country. They recognised that things had changed since we left, and a level of reconciliation had occurred. If the United States could move forward with Vietnam, so too could many of the people who once left.

While I was raised in the US and am proud to be American, Vietnam is my home. And though the country faced turmoil and conflict for much of the twentieth century, it is *finally* coming into its own. All these years later, I continue to be excited by the opportunities it offers.

INTRODUCTION

First-time visitors to Vietnam will often marvel at the traffic. Motorbikes, cars, buses and trucks all share the roads – and sometimes even the same lanes – and to the uninitiated, it appears that there are very few rules motorists follow.

They witness vehicles driving on the wrong side of the road, people driving motorbikes on the sidewalk, cars turning left at an intersection from the far-right lane and a range of other practices that would violate the rules of their home countries. But in Vietnam, traffic usually flows like water and reasonably well despite the organised chaos.

The real test for visitors (and even long-time residents) is crossing the street. Apart from a few areas in the central business districts, crossing signals are non-existent. And even where there are lights, motorbikes will obliviously whiz through. Afraid of getting run over, many visitors limit their walking tours to peripheral circles around the block. Sure, it's safer, but they definitely miss some interesting sites.

So how do you achieve what should be a very simple task? How do you avoid motorbikes, cars and buses all coming at you from various directions? How do you navigate a place where the rules are so different from other countries, if there are rules at all?

There is a secret to successfully crossing the street that usually works. Some intrepid visitors figure it out, while others are too scared of what they see.

It's actually fairly simple. The traffic in Vietnam flows like water, and drivers will usually go around pedestrians. But that only works if the pedestrian crosses the street with some confidence and at a steady pace. If they panic and stop in the middle of the street, they are likely to get hit.

The frenzy of Vietnam's traffic is a good metaphor for investing in the country. Investors have to be somewhat brave — it is a developing market, after all – and have patience. It can be frustrating at times. But if they understand the hazards and heed the lessons learned by others, it usually works out.

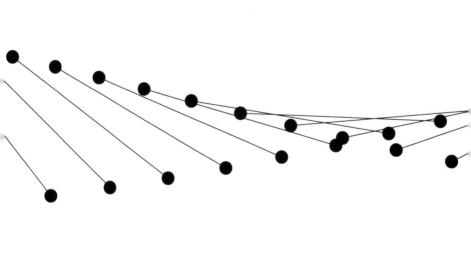

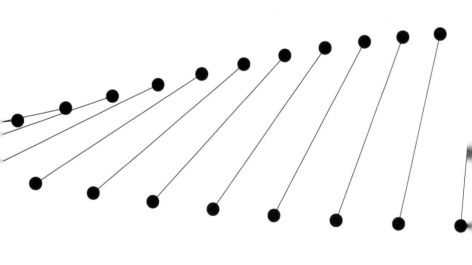

CHAPTER 1

WHY INVEST
IN VIETNAM

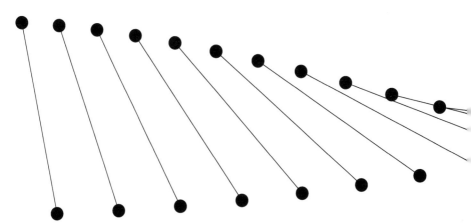

If you're reading this book, I assume that you have some interest in or knowledge of Vietnam. Perhaps you took a holiday to the country and were impressed by what you saw. Or you recently read some news about Vietnam and your interest has been piqued. Maybe you're a retail investor who owns shares in a fund like the one I manage.

In my role, I get to spend a fair amount of time standing in front of people talking about why they should invest in Vietnam (hopefully via VOF). In those meetings (or more recently, Zoom calls), I find that knowledge about Vietnam varies wildly. A diminishing minority still hold a view of the country during the war era – rebuilding from the devastation of decades of conflict. And while there are vestiges of the war still being dealt with, Vietnam has come a long way since then.

Vietnam is something of an enigma. It's a young country with a history that dates back centuries. It's a market economy governed by the Communist Party – one of the last five communist countries in the world. In terms of population, Vietnam ranks 15 in the world, while its economy ranks 36 as of 2020. This once closed-off country is now party to more free trade agreements (FTAs) than any other country in Southeast Asia. At the end of 2020, Vietnam signed an FTA with the United Kingdom, the 17th such agreement the country has entered into.

Why invest in Vietnam? It comes down to a few, very compelling, fundamental reasons.

1. A substantial population of nearly 100 million people, two-thirds of whom are below the age of 35 – it's the last significantly sized market in Asia to develop.

2. A fast-growing middle class of nearly 30 million, who are driving an economy that is based largely on the consumption of goods and services.

3. Asia's quick urbanisation rate, which is creating demand for new housing and infrastructure.

4. A growing manufacturing sector that is quickly transforming into the production hub of Southeast Asia thanks to low wages and a reasonably well-educated workforce.

5. Stability across a range of metrics, including currency, inflation, and government.

6. A government that is committed to fully integrating into the global economy and to continued economic reforms that attract investment and ultimately improve the lives of the Vietnamese people

To understand how Vietnam evolved so rapidly, a very brief review of its post-war history is probably in order.

The Vietnam War ended on April 30, 1975, when the People's Army of Vietnam rolled tanks through the gates of the South Vietnamese presidential palace in Saigon and raised their flag. The iconic photo of helicopters evacuating people from the US Embassy and from a nearby rooftop is how many people of a certain age recall that crazy and desperate day.

Known as the American War in Vietnam, its human costs were enormous. Estimates vary widely, but Vietnam has stated that two million civilians and more than one million military personnel died during the conflict. The US saw more than 58,000 servicemen killed in action, while its other allies, including Australia and South Korea, recorded another 6,000 dead. There were also casualties in the neighbouring countries of Cambodia and Laos. And let's not forget the hundreds of thousands who survived but were wounded, often with permanent injury. Needless to say, the scale of loss was almost incomprehensible, no matter whose side you were on.

The new communist government of a unified Vietnam set about nationalising and centralising the economy. As a result, the economy stagnated, inflation soared, and food shortages were common. It was during this period, from 1975–1979, that many Vietnamese people hailing primarily from the south left the country as political and/or economic refugees. My family were among them. An estimated 800,000 of those who left the country on boats arrived safely in a foreign country. Thousands more died at sea, the victims of pirates, storms, exposure, and unsafe boats.

What many people do not realise is that Vietnam went back to war in late 1978, not against a foreign superpower, but to drive the Khmer Rouge out of Cambodia. That conflict, which successfully ended the genocidal regime of Pol Pot (which officially lasted until 1989), saw a further 35,000 Vietnamese casualties. For nearly 50 years, Vietnam had essentially been in a state of war.

Why is that last point important? Because the war that most people think of did not suddenly end in 1975 – for Vietnam, it continued for another 14 years. As a result, the need to rebuild the country's physical infrastructure was huge. Besides this, the leaders were transitioning to a centrally planned economic model at a time when such philosophies were already falling out of favour and showing their deficiencies – the fall of the Berlin Wall and the demise of the Soviet Union to name a few.

By 1986, it had become clear that the things promised by a planned economy were not materialising. In fact, the lives of most Vietnamese people were not improving. That year, the government unveiled its *Doi Moi* policies, which translates to 'renovation', a series of far-reaching reforms aimed to transform the country into a socialist-oriented market economy. Included among the policies was Vietnam's first law on foreign investment, which provided the foundation for foreign companies and investors to come to the country.

Although it took some time (and numerous revisions) for the Doi Moi reforms to gain traction, the results today speak for themselves. Vietnam's economy is now thriving, and several billion dollars of foreign investment flows here every year.

Vietnam is now one of the most integrated countries in the global economy for the region, something that would have been unthinkable even 20 years ago. That integration process began in earnest in 1994, when the US normalised relations with Vietnam and lifted its trade embargo. The following year, Vietnam joined the Association of South East Asian Nations (ASEAN) and in 2007, it joined the World Trade Organization with the support of the US. Today, the country is signatory to many FTAs, including with the EU, Korea, and Japan, as well as part of the CPTPP (Comprehensive and Progressive Agreement for Trans-Pacific Partnership) and RCEP (Regional Comprehensive Economic

Partnership). This integration has been a critical factor in the relocation of manufacturing to the country and subsequent growth of exports, again driven primarily by foreign companies.

During the period 2009–2019, Vietnam's gross domestic product (GDP) grew by an average of nearly 7% per annum. In 2019, GDP rose 7% to reach $262bn, while GDP per capita reached $2,715. While the latter figure might seem small, there are two important things to note. First, in 2009 GDP per capita stood at $1,217 – in 1986, the year the Doi Moi reforms were announced, it stood at $422. Second, GDP per capita in HCMC and Hanoi was approximately $7,000.

In 2002, the World Bank estimated that 70% of the population lived below the poverty line; today, that figure stands at below 6%, mainly concentrated among the ethnic minorities who live in Vietnam's remote mountainous regions. Vietnam is credited for the speed at which it reduced poverty – one of the fastest reduction rates over the last 100 years.

GDP growth (%)

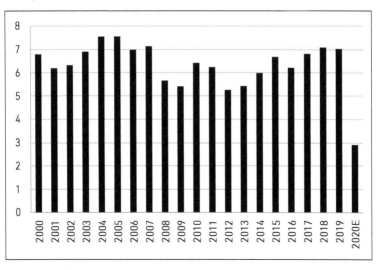

Source: General Statistics Office

GDP per capita (USD)

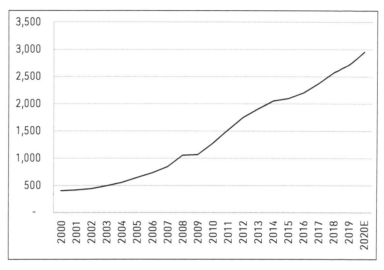

Source: General Statistics Office

Currency, inflation and interest rates

Vietnam's currency is the Vietnamese Dong (VND). In recent years, the VND has been fairly stable against the US Dollar (USD), but that has not always been the case. For many years, the State Bank of Vietnam (SBV) would devalue the currency, in a way that was similar to what the Chinese did with the Yuan. This resulted in fairly dramatic, periodic devaluations that were disruptive and reduced confidence in the currency.

But in 2016, the SBV instituted what our chief economist calls a gradual managed float (essentially a crawling PEG rate to the USD), which was designed to allow the VND to devalue in small increments over time and reduce the spread between the official and black-market exchange rates. Since then, the currency has been spared from the sharp devaluations of the past, and some economists believe that the VND is poised to start appreciating in 2021. At the end of December 2020, Vietnam had almost $100bn in reserves. This was well above the three-months' worth of imports threshold that international financial institutions such as the IFC and the World Bank suggest, and which economists look at as an indicator of currency stability. In addition, Vietnam has recorded five consecutive years of trade surpluses (as of December 2020).

USD/VND (2000-2020)

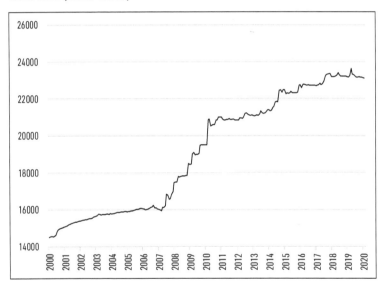

Source: Bloomberg

Well-controlled inflation has also been a significant contributor to Vietnam's recent growth. After peaking in 2011 at 18.58%, today inflation is fairly stable at around 3–4% per annum.

Consumer Price Index (%)

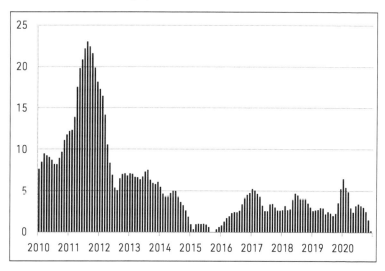

Source: General Statistics Office

Demographics, urbanisation and middle-class expansion

Vietnam's population is estimated to be around 97 million and is growing at a rate of about 1% a year. The population is young, with 67% under the age of 35, and relatively well educated. Thanks in part to the Jesuit missionaries who transcribed a form of ancient Chinese characters used in Vietnam into the Latin alphabet in the seventeenth century (with the French requiring its usage in the early twentieth century), Vietnam has a literacy rate of 95%.

Just over one-third (38%) of Vietnam's population live in cities. However, each year official figures show that migration to urban areas is occurring at 2–3% per annum – the highest rate in Asia. This trend is expected to continue for the medium term as more people seek better employment opportunities in places like HCMC, Hanoi, Danang and Haiphong.

China's experience in the twenty-first century offers a glimpse of what might happen here: today, 60% of China's population live in cities, up from 36% in 2000. If the same patterns hold, Vietnam's cities should prepare for significant growth.

Of course, urban migration puts pressure on existing infrastructure and public services, such as education, healthcare, housing, banking, and logistics. All of these are running to catch up with increasing demand – which is why we tend to focus on these sectors when we invest. Effectively, we like to focus on sectors that benefit from and/or contribute to the growth of the domestic economy.

The population is also becoming more affluent. Earlier I mentioned GDP per capita. On the basis of purchasing power parity, it is now over $7,000 per capita (to again use China as a point of reference, GDP PPP is $16,600 per capita). Vietnam's burgeoning middle class is expected to reach 30 million in the next few years – which is about half the population of the UK and larger than the entire population of Australia.

This group of consumers is spending across nearly every sector of Vietnam's vibrant economy. They are purchasing new homes and apartments (and everything needed to build and furnish them), as well as motorbikes and cars; securing private healthcare services and private schools for their kids; shopping for clothes, jewellery, and mobile phones; and flying domestically or abroad (when they can) on more frequent family vacations. This segment of the population is eager to improve their quality of life, and eager to spend their growing wages.

Social stability

Underpinning Vietnam's economic growth story is political and social stability. This is critical in a country like Vietnam, which, like China, is a one-party state. When there is only one political party, the government needs to constantly ensure that it remains relevant.

The Vietnamese people judge the relevancy of the government by their own circumstances. They ask, "are the people in government giving me the value I expect from them?" and "is my life improving?" And what they consider value is usually in the form of a job that allows them to feed and educate their children, access to healthcare, and infrastructure that allows them to get around more easily. Each of these elements needs to improve steadily over time so that the people can experience their benefits through a better quality of life. That is what keeps the social fabric strong.

Here is an example of what that means: it was not that long ago that Vietnam was a country that had to import food. In less than 20 years, Vietnam has gone from a famine-stricken country to one that exports a tremendous amount of food. Many people attribute this progress to land ownership, development of private enterprises, and the government's focus on improving people's lives.

Social instability tends to occur in countries experiencing high levels of inflation and unemployment. Those two issues do not presently exist in Vietnam.

Vietnam's political stability today stands in stark contrast to some of its neighbours, including Thailand, Malaysia, and even Hong Kong. Although the party sees political manoeuvring behind the scenes, that does not concern most people. In the end, the result is what matters to them, and that is a leadership team that governs by consensus and continually works to better the lives of the Vietnamese people.

The foreign investment story

Foreign direct investment (FDI) has played a crucial role in Vietnam's development. Between 2009 and 2019, disbursed FDI more than doubled from $7.6bn to $16.1bn.

FDI (2014-2020)

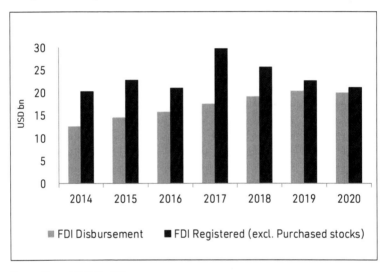

Source: General Statistics Office

As much as two-thirds of it is directed toward manufacturing, as foreign companies increasingly move production to Vietnam from places like China to broaden their supply chains and take advantage of lower labour costs (which are approximately one-third to one-half of China's). Vietnam's strategic location makes it ideal for producing goods for export, while its increasingly affluent populace makes it an attractive market in its own right. Furthermore, ongoing trade tensions between the US and China have made it necessary for manufacturers to look more carefully at their supply chains to ensure that they can continue to export to the US without fear of tariffs being imposed or otherwise getting tangled up in a geo-political conflict.

FDI is great for the economy, for the country as a whole, and for investors like VinaCapital. It is what I refer to as 'sticky money' – it is here to stay. While we would not invest in the multinational company establishing or expanding its operations in Vietnam, the spill-over effect presents opportunities. Here's how.

First, there is a mini real estate boom after a foreign investor buys land for their manufacturing plant. Companies that supply the plant may also choose to build factories or warehouses nearby. Infrastructure around the plant may need to be upgraded to support it. These create mini employment booms, as workers are hired to build factories, and then work in them. The factory is likely to import the latest machinery and equipment, which will increase the skills of the local workforce. The project creates a lot of value in the local area and as investors, we see great potential in this.

The opportunities lie in real estate – we will look at buying land nearby, for example – where homes will be built for the factory's future workforce. Or the opportunities may be in infrastructure – roads, bridges, electricity, water, and the materials necessary to build them, such as steel. Or they could be around consumers goods and services. The possibilities are almost endless.

Risks

By now, I hope you are convinced that the case for investing in Vietnam is compelling. However, no discussion about the subject can occur without addressing the very real risks that come with it. Investors face the same risks in Vietnam as they would in any other frontier or emerging market, and some of those risks bear mentioning.

For example, there is always a risk that inflation could get out of hand. This has happened at various points in the past, often triggered by high credit growth in conjunction with a depreciating currency and trade deficits – although the latter factor is unlikely these days, as Vietnam has run an enormous trade surplus since 2018. And while inflation has held steady at around 3–4% over the past few years, it was not that long ago that it was in the double digits. If left unchecked once again, inflation could lead to a depreciation of the local currency, the VND. In such cases, investments lose value.

Liquidity is another risk. If a company has listed on the stock market and it is not widely traded, you risk driving the share price down when you want to sell your position. If you have an investment in a private company, selling may be difficult, if it's even possible at all, due to a lack of interested parties.

The legal system and the ability to resolve disputes is another risk. Vietnam's laws and regulations are at an early stage in their development and are not yet well established. The local court system still has a way to go until it can provide the kind of dependability and impartiality of court systems in other countries. As a result, an aggrieved investor may face an unfair outcome in a legal dispute. Furthermore, foreign court judgements are rarely recognised in Vietnam. VOF, like many large companies, tends to require the use of arbitration centres in Singapore and Hong Kong, which can mitigate the risks, but sometimes has to use the arbitration centres in Vietnam, which, while much improved over the years, still cannot match the foreign centres' sophistication and impartiality.

There is a risk that the regulatory landscape changes in a way that is no longer friendly to foreign investors. We have seen that in many countries around the world. For example, not that long ago the Thai government imposed a 10% tax withholding on repatriation of capital for foreign investments, a move that predictably discouraged foreign investment. However, we do not see that as a likely scenario in Vietnam, given the government's recognition of the tremendous benefits brought by foreign investment.

The government could also arbitrarily seize or repatriate assets. And while some people may have the belief that a one-party state is apt to do such things, we have not seen that in Vietnam – the few isolated exceptions involved domestic businesses that purchased land incorrectly. Again, this is a very unlikely, although possible, scenario.

One final risk I will mention is a disruption to the business environment in the wake of a corruption scandal. Fraud, bribery, and corruption are relatively common in developing countries, including Vietnam. Sometimes business leaders begin to think they are above the law. And if they are leading businesses that are state-owned, the ramifications for misappropriating state funds, losing money, or not following the proper processes for land sales can be harsh, such as life in prison or even capital punishment.[1] VinaCapital and VOF

---

[1] "Vietnam's punishment for corrupt bankers: Death", *Washington Post*, 14 April 2015; and "Appeal court gives out death and life sentences in OceanBank case", *Vietnam Investment Review*, 5 May 2018.

maintain and adhere to stringent anti-corruption policies, and we go to great lengths to ensure that the businesses we invest in and deal with do the same. However, despite our best efforts, there remains a risk that someone with whom we do business could be implicated in corrupt activities. I note this because the current government has made rooting out corruption amongst officials a top priority, and it has had spill-over effects to the economy, particularly around real estate.

This list is not exhaustive, but it contains the things that every investor in the country must keep at the back of their mind and factor into their decisions. The key is to understand these risks and set the terms of investment accordingly.

Vietnam is a dynamic and exciting country, buzzing with entrepreneurialism and opportunities for both foreign and Vietnamese investors. The government continually works to improve the investment environment and to foster economic growth, but investors should never forget that Vietnam is still a developing country with its own unique characteristics, quirks, and risks.

Vietnam and Covid-19

When the idea for this book was first mentioned, one risk, Covid-19, didn't even exist – at least not in humans. Few people outside the public-health community would have predicted that a pandemic would sweep the world and essentially shut down much of it for nearly a year at the time of writing, and likely well into 2021.

In contrast to larger, wealthier countries (which for the most part have fumbled their response to Covid-19), Vietnam has drawn attention because of its effective management of the virus from the very start, back in late January 2020. Borders were progressively closed, contract tracing initiated, and central quarantine facilities opened – all of which minimised the spread of the virus in the community. The key to Vietnam's success likely lies in the mandatory 14-day quarantine in government-controlled facilities for those in contact with Covid patients as well as all inbound travellers. A very successful public information campaign that was covered by international media also played a significant role.

Flare-ups in Danang in late July 2020 and more recently in HCMC in November 2020 were similarly handled – the aggressive response not only stopped the spread of the disease but also its effect on the economy. Throughout the pandemic, Vietnam has never experienced the harsh lockdowns seen in other countries. Instead, there was a three-week period of 'mandatory social distancing' in April in which people who worked in offices worked from home, dining in restaurants was not permitted, and a range of businesses, such as gyms, bars, and cinemas, were closed. Face masks were required in public areas, and violators were fined the equivalent of about $8 (I was fined one morning for not wearing a mask during my daily jog). Public mask use is still required to this day.

The results speak for themselves: fewer than 1,500 confirmed cases and less than three-dozen deaths as of December 2020. Some may question the accuracy of these numbers, but it should be noted that Vietnam is not China – the internet is open, and there has been no online gossip surrounding the situation. Additionally, a few foreign public-health research entities are located in Vietnam, notably the Oxford University Clinical Research Unit, the director of which is on the record in international media as verifying and complimenting Vietnam's effective response. More importantly, Vietnamese people had some of the highest confidence in their government's response to the pandemic in the world, according to a survey conducted in 2020. As such, Vietnamese citizens have a high level of compliance with their government's requests and warnings.

It should be noted that factories continued to operate throughout the pandemic – as long as safety measures were implemented, that is. This allowed people to work and earn wages. The Vietnamese government also implemented some stimulus measures to help boost the economy. As a result, the economy has forged ahead. Retail sales have bounced back to pre-pandemic rates, exports are up, and with GDP growth of 2.9% for 2020, Vietnam will rank as one of the few countries with an economy still expanding. The stock market, as measured by the VN Index, was up 15.2% in 2020, or 65% from its lowest point in March 2020.

The government's deft handling of the outbreak further bolstered the confidence of foreign investors, who were impressed by both the public-health actions to control the virus and the fact that Vietnam remained 'open for business' when many other countries were not.

All that said, we cannot ignore that many people in Vietnam have been greatly affected by the economic consequences of Covid-19. Tourism – which accounts directly for 10% of the GDP and almost 20% indirectly – remains shut, save for domestic travellers. Hotels, airlines, and a whole range of related businesses are hurting. However, if there is one word to describe Vietnam and the Vietnamese people, it is resilient. I have no doubt that those and other sectors will recover once the global pandemic is brought under control.

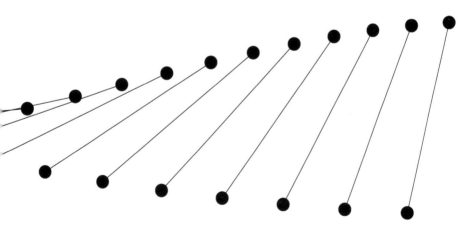

CHAPTER 2

HOW TO INVEST IN VIETNAM

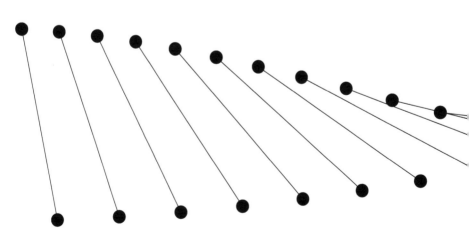

The case for investing in Vietnam should now be clear and you may be wondering, "how can I participate in this dynamic market?"

There are several ways foreigners can invest. Legally, foreigners can set up accounts with a Vietnamese stockbroker or securities firm and directly trade listed equities. The process for doing so, however, is more complex than the average retail investor living in the UK may have the tolerance for. They could also buy shares in one of Vietnam's exchange-traded funds (ETFs) through a broker at home. Better yet, they could purchase shares in one of the handful of closed- or open-ended funds that focus on Vietnam, like VOF or the Forum One – VCG Partners Vietnam Fund (VVF), a UCITS-compliant fund also managed by VinaCapital. Most of these funds invest in listed equities.

A brief history of Vietnam's stock markets

We often refer to 'Vietnam's stock market', but there are actually three exchanges: the Ho Chi Minh Stock Exchange, which constitutes the Vietnam Index (VN Index), the Hanoi Stock Exchange, and the Unlisted Public Company Market (UPCoM), which is actually part of the Hanoi Stock Exchange. Like the country as a whole, the listed equity market has come a long way in a fairly short amount of time.

The Ho Chi Minh City Securities Trading Center (HoSTC) first banged its gong – rather than rang a bell – on 28 July 2000 with just two stocks: Refrigeration Electrical Engineering Joint Stock Corporation (REE) and Saigon Cable and Telecommunication Material Joint Stock Company (SACOM). Seven years later, the centre was renamed the Ho Chi Minh Stock Exchange (HOSE). By the end of 2007, there were 507 types of listed securities on the exchange, including six foreign-owned entities and 366 bonds.

The Hanoi Securities Trading Centre was set up in March 2005. It was renamed the Hanoi Stock Exchange in 2009. Later that year, the Unlisted Public Company Market (UPCoM) was launched.

The Ho Chi Minh Stock Exchange is where the blue chips are listed. There were 403 stocks listed there, and these accounted for about 90% of the combined market capitalisation of Vietnam's three bourses (as of December 2020). The Hanoi Stock Exchange has 353 stocks trading there, although it is also home to Vietnam's nascent bond market. UPCoM is where newly equitised SOEs now list prior to migrating to the Ho Chi Minh Stock Exchange (provided they meet a range of criteria) as well as other smaller, newly public companies. In total, UPCoM has 907 listed companies.

As of 31 December 2020, the capitalisation of Vietnam's three bourses stood at nearly $229bn, with average daily trading reaching $313m.

Market capitalisation 2010–2020 (USDm)

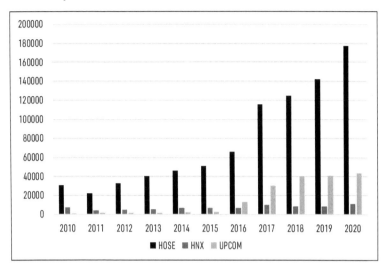

Source: Bloomberg

Most of the companies listed on the stock markets were originally SOEs. Over the years, they privatised (or 'equitised', as it is called here), restructured and eventually listed. Some of these privatisations, especially of entities that are core to Vietnam's society and economy, like Vinamilk (Vietnam's largest dairy company), have provided great opportunities for foreign investors to participate in the country's economic growth. Over the past ten years, a fair number of private companies have also listed on the stock exchanges.

Despite the progress the stock market has made in recent years, there continues to be room for further development. Foreign ownership limits (FOLs) are probably the biggest hindrance preventing greater investment from international institutions. For most listed companies, foreigners can own no more than 49% of the shares of a company (or 30% in banks). In 2015, the government changed the law to allow most companies to remove the FOLs (exceptions: banks and companies operating in selected strategic sectors). The onus is on the company to take action to do so. To date, approximately 50 listed companies have entirely removed or expanded (i.e., allow more but still limit foreign investment) their FOLs. This has created a situation where stakes owned by foreign investors trade off-market at a premium.

The next catalyst for growth of Vietnam's stock markets is graduation to emerging market status. In 2018, expectations were high that Vietnam would make MSCI's watch list for emerging market status. That did not happen, as MSCI identified a number of issues, FOLs chief among them, that Vietnam needs to address in order to 'move up'. But once the country graduates, I would expect a surge of additional foreign investment in the stock market, as most international funds are precluded from investing in frontier markets, which Vietnam remains today.

From 2019 until now, the focus of investors, and particularly foreign investors, has been on listed equities. This is largely because the valuations were inexpensive and the economy has demonstrated continued stability and vibrancy. Although valuations in terms of price-to-earnings ratio (P/E), price-to-sales ratio (P/S) and EBITDA (earnings before interest, taxes, depreciation, and amortisation) have climbed, they still trail those of regional markets such as Indonesia, Malaysia, and the Philippines.

Since 2007, I have managed the VinaCapital Vietnam Opportunity Fund (VOF), an investment trust listed on the London Stock Exchange's Main Market, a member of the FTSE 250, and one of the largest Vietnam-focused funds. I also serve as chief investment officer of VinaCapital, an investment management company founded in 2003 which manages around $3bn in assets across a full range of classes as of December 2020.

VOF is unique among the Vietnam-focused funds in that in addition to holding listed equities, it also does private-equity investments, participates in the equitisation of SOEs, and provides debt and financing to help companies grow. This active, multi-asset approach gives investors exposure to more than just the stock market, but also to some of Vietnam's most promising private companies. In addition to being the only Vietnam-focused fund that pays a dividend and has an active (and tax-efficient) share buy-back programme – over $350m as of December 2020 – this formula has generated superior returns for investors over the long term.

We focus on companies that are participating in and driving the domestic consumption story. We are sector agnostic. We have invested in milk companies and liquor companies, hospitals and schools, property developers and construction companies, airlines and airports. To varying degrees, all of these sectors are seeing sustained growth. Of course, not all companies are equal. Some are better managed than others. And that is where our experience in the market and our strong network comes into play.

As the valuations of listed equities have risen, investors have started to turn their focus toward private investment opportunities with the belief that one can access these companies at a lower valuation due to these companies having a different set of risks, such as liquidity and transparency. From the investee or sponsor's perspective, private equity is viewed as an option because credit is actually still difficult for businesses to access. Although flush with liquidity, the Vietnam banking system is still working through non-performing loans and deleveraging, resulting in limited credit growth. Although that dynamic needs to and will likely change as time goes by, it does provide opportunities for investors like VOF and others.

What will we not invest in? There are strategic sectors that are restricted for foreign investors, such as those relating to national security. We also tend not to invest in Vietnamese companies that are primarily export-driven, or those involved in the production of commodities. Export-driven businesses have a lot of competition from around South East Asia, China, and other parts of the world. There are also too many uncontrollable external factors that can negatively affect the value of the enterprise, with few options to mitigate them when they arise. In Chapter 4, I go into more detail about why we tend not to invest in those types of companies.

We also apply a rigorous set of ESG criteria to our existing and new investments, especially around the issues of energy use/production, water usage, and waste disposal. We retain the services of a noted international ESG consultancy, which we use to evaluate potential investments. Some of the businesses we choose to invest in may not adhere to international standards, but as long as their management is open to making change, we will work with them to improve their practices and processes, which ultimately adds to the value of the enterprise.

How do we make money for our investors?

Whenever we make an investment, our plan is usually to exit within three to five years, either through a trade sale to a strategic buyer or by taking the company onto the stock market. However, a listing does not necessarily mean that we will dispose of our stake. If a company continues to perform well after we have taken it public, we will sometimes hold on to the investment for longer than five years. A good example of this is Hoa Phat Group, Vietnam's largest steelmaker, which we invested in and took public in 2007, and in which we still maintain a large stake today. In fact, many of the listed stocks in our portfolio started out as private-equity investments many years before.

When we make private-equity investments, we prefer to take minority positions, between 10% and 40% of the company. A majority or control position creates a world of complexities around management and leadership changes that we would rather not deal with, nor are we necessarily suited to deal with, although there have been some cases where it has become necessary to do so to increase the value of the investment. Some of those scenarios will be described later in the book.

Trade sales are our preferred exit. Our shares, together with those of the sponsor, enable us to sell a controlling stake to a strategic buyer. Selling a controlling stake in a business typically enables us to command a premium over selling a smaller stake. Sometimes that premium can be 15%, and sometimes it can be 100% over the prevailing market price.

We know from experience that strategic buyers value three elements. When we make an investment with a view to a trade sale, we look at companies that have at least two of these three elements:

1. **Brand equity:** Do they produce products that have strong brand recognition and value?

2. **Distribution channels:** Have they developed a wide distribution channel in Vietnam, beyond the main cities?

3. **Scalability:** Do they have manufacturing scalability, whether it is fixed assets, people or land? If you have factories sitting on land that cannot be expanded, it is not scalable.

Multinationals have two choices when they come to Vietnam. They can either build a business organically or acquire an existing one. Our thesis is that in the current environment, where the cost of capital for these multinationals in their home country is low, the likelihood that they will spend the time and money to organically build a business is low. Plus, there is also no guarantee that they will be successful in doing so – more than one international company has tried and failed. Another consideration is that their sector may have legal restrictions on foreign companies (e.g., retail, pharmaceuticals, etc.). Because these multinationals tend to have ample cash and are impatient, their entry point into the market usually comes via buying an established business with a track record, rather than growing a business organically.

Naturally, buying stakes in businesses carries its own set of risks. As a long-time investor in Vietnam, I have developed the following 20 'rules' for investing. They are based on my experiences and those of my colleagues, as well as others in the market. I initially put these together to guide my team as they evaluate potential investments, primarily in the private-equity space. As with most rules, there are exceptions. But these rules can be considered a guide for how to successfully cross the street without getting grazed or hit by oncoming traffic.

These 20 rules primarily address issues that arise when evaluating and making an investment, as well as factors that need to be considered and documented. The final few rules relate to exits, especially those that might come under pressure.

The fundamentals:

1. Ensure that management's interests and key shareholders' interests align with your own.

2. A carrot without a stick is useless.

3. Trust in the management; their experience is key.

The 'nevers':

4. Never invest in a subsidiary.

5. Never invest in a greenfield hotel...

6. ...or build a hospital.

7. Avoid export businesses and body shops.

8. Never buy anything from another 'healthy' fund or financial investor.

9. Never invest in a company belonging to your friend... or your enemy.

10. No money out!

Trust but verify: the importance of due diligence and documentation:

11. Do not believe in the memories of entrepreneurs.

12. Get official documents for all transactions.

13. Perform health and background checks on key executives.

14. Husbands and wives do get divorced – consider it carefully when investing in a family business.

15. When in doubt, put it in the assumption section of the letter of intent or term sheet.

16. Any promise can be broken if it is not written down in a signed document.

Getting out: exit considerations:

17. Always have an exit clause, even if you have to pay a penalty.

18. Control your money to leverage your position.

19. Think three times when exercising a convertible loan.

20. Don't take control; use the drag-along right.

To a reader living in the developed world, many of these rules will seem obvious. But seemingly experienced international investors still overlook these rules – it happens more often than you might expect. And that underscores one of my key points: investors unfamiliar with Vietnam, its business culture, and how things are done here, would be well served to partner with those who are familiar with these things. While there is no fool-proof way to make an investment a success, adhering to these rules certainly increases the likelihood of doing so.

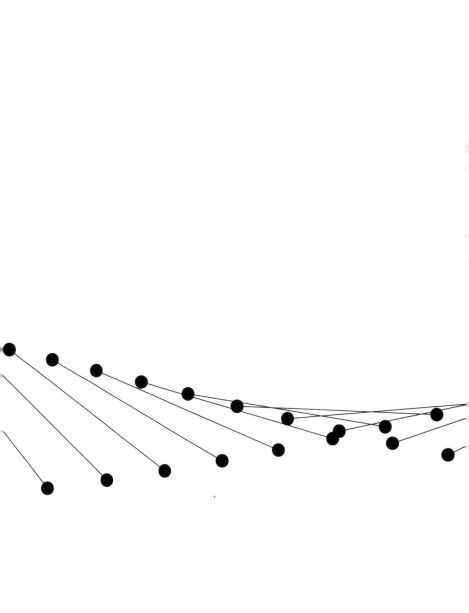

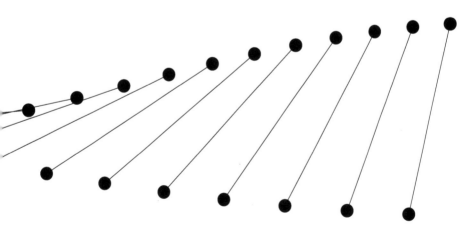

CHAPTER 3

THE FUNDAMENTALS

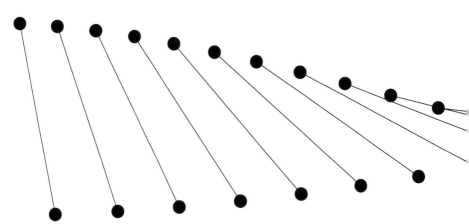

VOF is sector agnostic. We will invest in almost any company with growth potential that benefits from Vietnam's impressive domestic growth and consumption story – with a few exceptions described later. That means we could be investing in developers of townhouses and apartments, producers of ice cream and biscuits, hospitals, schools, steel, banks – you name it.

But no matter the company or the sector, there are three fundamental factors we have to consider as we look at a potential investment: is management's interests aligned with ours? Can we really trust them to deliver on what they promise? And what can we do if they fail to deliver?

Rule 1: Ensure that management's interests and key shareholders' interests align with your own

First and foremost, we want to ensure that the interests of the sponsor and/or management of the company in which we want to invest are aligned with our own. We want to make sure that the existing team remain fully invested in the future growth of the company once we are on board.

This seems straightforward. You would think that someone selling a stake in his or her company would have the same objectives as you, the investor: growth and a profitable exit. And while that is usually the case, that's not always been so.

In the early 2000s, there were approximately 15,000 SOEs. Some were reasonably well-managed, others not so much. But there was a lot of capital tied up in these businesses, and the government realised that equitising (or privatising) them would enable it to mobilise capital for fiscal purposes as well as for hard and soft infrastructure investments. It encouraged these businesses to become more competitive for human and financial resources, and to produce goods and services at prices that would generate reasonable demand. Key to this initiative was enfranchising the management to become shareholders and owners of these SOE businesses, which they had been running for years or even decades.

The government realised that aligning its interests as shareholders in the enterprises with those of their management was key to enhancing shareholder value, strengthening the balance sheet, and reducing 'leakages'. The view was that management would not be motivated to maximise the economics of a company if it was completely owned by the government. Decisions around issues such as long-term capital investments were made with less-than-ideal terms and conditions, leading to an inefficient use of human resources, equity, and debt capital. These inefficiencies often led to losses, which in turn led to government bailouts and more subsidised debt, all while employees enjoyed coffees all morning long before starting work at mid-day. There were few consequences for management or staff for inefficiencies or lacklustre performance.

Some SOE employees were actually quite creative – just not in the right way. There were many examples of executives of these enterprises creating family businesses to provide services to the SOE. For instance, a family-run distribution company would be ideal to help distribute the goods produced by the very SOEs the executives ran. Another example relates to friends or family of an SOE executive setting up a business to sell the inputs necessary to produce the goods made by the SOE.

One of my very first investments in Vietnam was in a fish-processing company that had recently equitised, with the government still the majority shareholder. Upon visiting the plant in the Mekong Delta, it became clear to us that more than half of the inputs (raw fish) came from the fish farms owned by the families of SOE executives. As such, the CEO was always able to guarantee a 10% gross margin! Needless to say, we had no comfort around the SOE's ability to purchase inputs at the lowest possible price, and I asked my team to exit the business completely.

As of 2020, this company languishes on the UPCoM, a far cry from when it was listed on the Ho Chi Minh Stock Exchange and as a darling of the market. Once investors understood that there was no alignment of interest with the management, the share price started to fall. Today, it trades at a price significantly below par, which for all listed companies in Vietnam is VND10,000 (or about 44 US cents).

While the genesis of this rule comes from the equitisation of SOEs, it applies equally to private companies. Most of our investments are in medium-to-large sized private companies where the founder is still active in the day-to-day business. They are talking to investors like us to help them further build their company, and in the process of doing that, make more money. They have already achieved a certain level of success but have likely reached their limit in terms of growing their business with the resources and experience available to them, with regard to both financial and human capital, and they are interested in expanding.

The founder is likely on the same page as you, at least in respect to the ultimate outcome. As the investor, we want to ensure that the founder remains active in the business. But alignment of interests goes beyond the founder or CEO. What about the other shareholders, who may be family members of the founder? Or the members of the board of directors? Or those in the C-suite? Just as with SOEs, alignment of interests must be gauged at several levels in a company.

Over the years, our due diligence exercises have uncovered numerous examples of a range of internal conflicts of interest at private-sector companies and SOEs that would give any credible institutional investor pause – provided they discovered them. Normally, conflicts of interest lead to a disalignment of interests. Just as with the fish-processing company described earlier, there are many examples – some of which we found and others that are widely known in the industry – of similar conflicts of interest that can complicate matters and potentially make an attractive investment much less so. Leakage can take many forms, including:

- A beer company where its distributors were owned and operated by company executives.

- A food company which sourced its key raw material from an offshore company that happened to be owned by a board member.

- A high-profile company where it is widely known that every purchasing order includes a 5–20% kickback.

- A large conglomerate where the chances of employment are higher if a candidate provides 'consideration' to the human resources department decision maker.

In short, there can be a number of 'accepted practices' entrenched in a company that do not support an external investor's interests. In the beer company, the new owners found that distribution costs kept going up even though revenue was declining. The food company illustrates how the costs of both input and output can be factors for leakage in the company. The high-profile company with kickbacks embedded in purchase orders certainly does not seem too interested in controlling costs. Meanwhile, the large conglomerate is not necessarily hiring the best candidates for jobs, just those willing to pay the price of admission.

Real estate development companies can be particularly ripe for leakage. When they purchase land, they may be purchasing it from an individual or entity associated with the company, either an executive or a company run by a related party, for example. The person or entity selling the land to the developer may have marked up the price by 10–20% to cover the 'unofficial' costs they incurred acquiring the property, such as the cost of relocating residents or businesses, obtaining documentation, or other forms of 'coffee money' that are commonly paid in real estate transactions. These expenses, however, cannot be documented, as receipts are not usually provided. Of course, not all developers engage in such practices, although it is known to be a relatively common business practice.

These examples illustrate just how deep into an organisation an investor should look to ensure that there is an alignment of interests. If the C-suite is approving a large capital expenditure, one must be certain that the contractors, consultants and other suppliers that are hired are legitimately independent – the transaction is at arm's-length. From what company is the IT department buying new laptops – a credible, independent supplier or a company run by the department head's sister-in-law? The opportunities for leakage run throughout a company!

There are ways to prevent these kinds of situations. What elements do we look for (and what do we recommend) to ensure that a *misalignment* of interests is minimised?

1. **Management team are shareholders.** The C-suite needs to have a meaningful stake in the company to ensure that they are acting in the best interests of all shareholders, including themselves. The stakes should comprise of a significant percentage of their personal wealth, and ideally, should be long-term oriented.

2. **Rotate managers every 2–3 years.** This gives managers the opportunity to learn about different parts of the operation, while also reducing the likelihood that they will become so entrenched so as to find ways to 'work the system'.

3. **Pay market-based, competitive compensation.** Far too many companies pay their executives low salaries with the understanding that they will have opportunities to supplement them by 'working the system'. The fixed salary should be competitive, and the variable portion of it should be based on meaningful key performance indicators (KPIs).

4. **Forced vacation.** Just as banks in many parts of the world now require certain levels of staff to take one or two weeks of leave and not take calls or answer emails as a way to prevent fraud, Vietnamese companies would be well served to do the same, even if not required by law.

It is unlikely that you will ever be able to root out all of these types of activities, so the key is to make sure everyone in the organisation is headed in the right direction. That can be achieved via employee stock-ownership programmes or option plans (ESOPs), which a number of Vietnamese companies offer, although they are structured differently than in other countries. In Vietnam, companies tend to go overboard in their awards to staff, perhaps as a way to balance out less-than-competitive salaries. ESOPs are also not accounted for in the financial statement in the same way as they are in the West and there is little long-term thinking behind them.

How have we addressed these issues when we have identified them?

First, we push for a large stock plan for executives – we want them to benefit along with us. With respect to ESOPs for other employees, we push to have them structured with long-term interests (e.g., vest over time, meeting targets, etc.) and for those shares to be liquid. Second, paying employees market-competitive salaries should lower the likelihood that certain staff may feel the need to supplement their pay by working the system. Concurrent with both of those should be a no-tolerance policy for operating related businesses, for taking kickbacks of any kind, or otherwise acting with questionable ethics.

The discovery of some issues is not necessarily a deal-killer. There are degrees of issues, and some of these practices are ingrained in the local business culture. The key is whether management is open to addressing the issues we identify. If they are, that bodes well. If they are not, or they ignore your recommendations, you are likely to have problems. That is why it is important to identify these weaknesses during the financial and legal due diligence stage and ask for these changes as a condition precedent to disbursement. Otherwise, the strength of the recommendation may become less effective once you have invested. Our ultimate aim is that the creation of value for all shareholders is the top priority and motivator, not individual interests.

The takeaways

- We want a manager to have equity in the business – and not just a token amount, but something that comprises of a significant part of their personal wealth. And their stake isn't given to them for free – they have to pay for their shares, so they feel the same level of pain other investors do if things do not go as planned.

- We never lose sight of the fact that we are ultimately investing capital in a company because we believe it will generate a good return for *our* shareholders. Generating returns for our shareholders is our primary focus, and we expect the same kind of focus from the leaders of the companies in which we invest.

- Alignment of interest is not only important between the management team and shareholders; it is also important between fund managers and *their* shareholders. There have been cases where fund managers' interests were not aligned with those of their own shareholders by making, for example, decisions that were detrimental to the fund's net asset value in the short and long term. There have also been reports of fund managers taking kickbacks for their investment decisions, front running, and, even worse, selling their personal shares back to the fund. I would encourage potential fund investors to do proper due diligence before they invest, and ask third parties about transactions that do not seem proper. But do keep in mind that the competitive nature of the industry in Vietnam, and in the region, presents ample opportunities for the spread of unsubstantiated or untrue rumours.

Rule 2: A carrot without a stick is useless

When we invest in a company, we prefer to take what we call significant minority stakes – large enough to make a difference but not in control. We typically make investments with a three- to five-year horizon, and over the course of the investment, we expect to see progress towards our goal of being able to exit with a minimum internal rate of return (IRR) of 20%.

To reach that goal, we usually set one or more of three key growth performance targets into our deals. These three targets – revenue, profit, and EBITDA – can all be measured on an annual basis, or on a three-year cumulative basis. These commitments are discussed with the sponsor and memorialised in the term sheet and final investment documentation.

These targets may be aggressive, but that will be reflected in how much we pay to take a stake. Ultimately, however, the CEO or founder must commit to these performance targets before we invest. It's an important alignment measure.

If a business's future growth is a carrot, we have to chase it with a stick – or in our case, four sticks. These are the penalties we include in our deal terms to ensure that there are ramifications for the sponsor for not fulfilling the commitment he or she made to us. To safeguard our investment, we typically negotiate the inclusion of four downside protections we have the option of exercising if commitments are not met:

1. A **cash rebate**, where the sponsor returns some of the principal (plus interest) to us;

2. A **share top-up**, whereby we are given more shares in the company – we have a bigger stake for the same amount of principal;

3. A **put option**, which allows us to sell our block of shares back to the sponsor or company, with a minimum IRR of 20–30%; and

4. **Drag-along rights**, under which the sponsor gives us enough of his stake so that we can assemble a controlling stake, which we could then sell to a strategic buyer.

If a company's performance is not going to plan, and there is no sign that things will improve due to market conditions or an unwillingness by management to change direction, we will not hesitate to exercise one of these options. First and foremost, however, we want to make every effort to bring the sponsor back to the table and work to find a mutually agreeable and beneficial solution – something that might only happen if we threaten to use a stick.

A rebate is the cleanest penalty to exercise – we get some of our money back but retain the same stake. There is a mathematical formula behind how much we might get refunded, but it essentially boils down to this: if the company met only 90% of the target, we would get back 10% of our investment plus interest.

Under the share top-up penalty, we would receive more shares for little to no additional cost based on a similar formula. The share top-up may seem illogical – why would we want more shares in a company that isn't performing as expected? This penalty as well as the others are meant to bring people to the table, to work through the problems and hopefully get things back on track. In other words, we may waive the penalty in return for substantive changes.

In contrast, if we must exercise a penalty, the put option is our preferred course of action. We sell back our entire stake to the sponsor at the original price, receiving our principal and a minimum IRR of 20–25% and exit the investment. Unfortunately, all too often the sponsor or company will not have the funds to pay as they have been spent for other purposes, legitimate or not. In private companies, effectuating a put option is fairly simple – there is no due diligence and if the company does not have the funds available to pay us out, the founder is able to use personal assets to do so. With a larger company planning to list, exercising this option would entail the company doing a treasury share purchase, which would require shareholder approval, drawing attention to an issue they would probably prefer few outsiders to know about.

Not long ago, we exercised a put option with one of our investees because they consistently missed their targets and we had little confidence that they would be willing to work with us to do what we believed was necessary to turn the business around. While they were not in a position to return the amounts owed in one payment, we worked with them on a short-term payment plan to return our funds – this was the best outcome for all parties involved, given the circumstances.

Drag-along rights allow us to assemble a controlling stake in the company, which would then enable us to potentially sell to a strategic buyer by 'dragging along' the sponsor and the shares he or she owns. Under this scenario, we would work with the sponsor to make improvements to the business so that we could ultimately exit. As I mentioned earlier, when we invest, we usually take minority stakes. But those are not as attractive to strategic buyers as controlling stakes, for which they tend to pay a nice premium. At the very least, we would want to sell a 51% stake. A 66% stake, which is a super-majority required by law to approve changes such as those to the registered capital or the corporate structure, can usually command a significant premium.

While drag alongs are complex, requiring due diligence, bankers and time, they are our second preferred penalty as they result in a financial win-win scenario – both ourselves and the sponsor benefit. However, the sponsor may need some time to fully appreciate that, as they may feel they were 'forced' to sell the company they had built from the ground up.

Exercising a downside protection usually results from missing a performance commitment. However, there is one other scenario where we may have an opportunity to exercise the drag along, and that is when we receive an offer for our stake which surpasses an agreed minimum enterprise value which enables us to sell at a significant premium. Coincidentally, when one of our investees missed their targets, we received an offer from a third party that valued our stake at three times our investment, far surpassing the minimum valuation, and enabling the drag along to kick in.

We want to encourage the sponsor to do what is required so that we all can eventually enjoy the carrot. But there cannot be an imbalance between the two – that causes demotivation. This is why whenever we are in a situation where we have the option to exercise a penalty, we first make every effort to bring the sponsor back to the table and work to find a mutually agreeable and beneficial solution.

The takeaways

- The downside protections we negotiate in our private-equity deals are an important and effective way to mitigate risk and ensure that our investees understand that we expect to see the results agreed to – we all want to end up in a position where we can eventually enjoy the carrot.

- There have to be ramifications for not performing as agreed, otherwise the investor will be left chasing promises that are unlikely to be kept.

- However, there must be balance between the carrot and stick – an imbalance can cause demotivation.

Rule 3: Trust in the management; their experience is key

It should probably go without saying that you should trust the people in whose company you are investing. Obviously, you're not going to invest with someone you don't trust. In general, we define a trusted management team as one that can develop a reasonable business plan, can execute it, and will not steal from the business. This rule also refers more specifically to a CEO's ability to fulfil the performance commitments we ask them to make as part of our investment.

Remember, over the course of our three- to five-year investment, we typically ask that management commits to delivering on either one or more of the following three key growth performance targets: revenue, profit, and EBITDA. These can be measured on an annual basis, or on a three-year cumulative basis.

The earliest test of trust usually comes when we first look at a company's business plan. We want to see something that is reasonable, with ambitious yet realistic projections, so that we can be confident that it can be executed.

Sometimes we will be given a very 'frothy' business plan, prepared by a management team who are focused on driving up the value of the business to lure the investor in. Once hooked, they may tell the investor the truth about the business, at which point it is too late.

Trust goes beyond the initial investment – it is something that must be checked over a relationship's duration. As active investors, we regularly engage with our private-equity investees and we may even have a seat on the board. If we see that a company is having difficulty meeting the agreed upon targets, first and foremost we want to work with management to identify the issues preventing this from happening and find solutions. As long as the issues are legitimate and solvable, we want to find ways to make things work.

Where we learned our lesson

In 2014, we invested in a small food and beverage (F&B) company located in the north of Vietnam that operated in a fast-growing segment of the market. Although the market was dominated by one company, the growth was so robust that it was clear it could support several players. We knew something about this business because we had been an early investor in the company that now dominates the market. This new company asked us to invest because they had a capital crisis – their cash flow could not service their debt.

Shortly after investing, it became clear that the issues were greater than they first appeared. Unsurprisingly, the management team was unable to meet the performance commitments they made to us.

What were our options? We couldn't ask for our cash back, because they had no cash. That also ruled out the put option. We couldn't drag them along, because nobody was going to buy the company in the condition it was in at that time. We exercised the share top-up penalty, and as a result, we suddenly found ourselves in the control seat.

We replaced the CEO with someone who was highly regarded for the work he did as a marketer at the company's biggest competitor. His reputation was solid. However, we overestimated his ability to manage the other core areas that we would expect a CEO to be skilled at managing. Primarily, CEOs need to:

1. **Know about sales and marketing.**

2. **Be knowledgeable about production**; what it costs to produce the product and how it is distributed.

3. **Know the financials**, including the cash and working capital/cash flow, long-term capital, and how they borrow money and service debt; as well as investment in terms of the returns on the machinery and land they buy, the buildings, and so on.

4. **Be knowledgeable about human resources** and who is being hired to do what.

5. **Have government and social relationships.** If you don't have government relationships in Vietnam, your business will fail. Social relationships are critical to building the business and include having a network comprised of other business leaders, being active in industry associations, and even knowing the business media and how they work.

While we don't expect CEOs to be experts in all of the above, we do want them to have a firm grasp of each area. The new CEO we installed at the F&B company ticked the first box and had some helpful social relationships, but he was not able to meet the other criteria.

The CEO did a great job at rebranding the company's products. However, a combination of creating a portfolio of products that was too expansive and a lack of proper cash-management systems led to further fiscal weaknesses. Ultimately, a senior member of my team became the acting CEO and over the course of a few years, was able to restructure the company's finances and improve performance. VOF was able to sell its stake to a Vietnamese financial and strategic buyer in 2020 with a good return.

What does 'trust' really mean?

How do I judge whether I can trust management? I have a few simple criteria:

1. **No stealing from the company.** That should be a given, but many CEOs of private companies will use company resources for personal purposes, such as supporting their real estate investments, gambling habits, and/or other vices.

2. **Don't create conflicts of interest.** It should be clear that they are looking after the interests of the company and the company's shareholders, not its subsidiaries or related entities.

3. **Transact at arm's-length.** Too often, deals are done with related parties or otherwise don't pass the smell test of being ethical.

There is a large, successful construction company in Vietnam that made a reputation for itself by doing good-quality work and delivering projects on time – no small feat in Vietnam! This attracted the attention of many investors, both Vietnamese and international, including us.

This company's construction services were constantly in demand, and it had a significant backlog of work. At some point, the sponsor decided to set up a few subsidiaries whereby the main company would hold less than 50%. Who held the rest? Mostly members of the board of directors and board of management of the main company, plus a few third-party investors!

This created obvious conflicts of interest. The subsidiary was used as a sub-contractor, but it also competed against the larger company for projects. If 'good' projects were brought to the main, larger company, would they somehow get passed on to the smaller subsidiary?

A major external shareholder (who had a seat on the board) took issue with this arrangement and "repeatedly questioned … [the board] on serious issues leading to a conflict of interests, related party transactions, resource use and the reputation of the larger group."[2] They further noted that in 2015, the after-tax profit of the subsidiary was equivalent to 11% of that of the larger company, but that in 2019, that figure jumped to 51%. The shareholders attempted to mount a boardroom coup, starting a protracted battle for control of the company. In 2020, it looked as if the parties had reached some sort of agreement after the company's annual general meeting, but by the end of the year, the chairman resigned, as did another long-time member of the board.

This is a clear example where personal interests trumped those of shareholders of the larger company, whose stock price has been battered by the issue. We saw this situation develop early on and tried to convince the sponsor to stay focused on the main company, but that fell on deaf ears. It was explained to us that the reason for setting up these subsidiaries was to motivate executives. It was thought that by providing executives with shares in these smaller businesses rather than with the main company, that they would take long-term decisions and views; in other words, they were attempting to align their interests with the main company or sponsor.

Why not give these executives shares in the main company? These executives recognised that their contributions to it were diluted by the results of many other departments and projects. Hence, they convinced the sponsor to allow them to set up various subsidiaries and have direct ownership alongside the sponsor.

In order for us to remain aligned with the sponsor, we took an equivalent stake in the largest subsidiary, and tried to convince the sponsor to merge the subsidiary into the main company – a move that would allow the subsidiary's executives as well as

---

2 *Saigon Dau Tu*, 20 October 2020.

the sponsor to acquire additional shares of the main company through a share swap. Needless to say, this plan did not pan out. The sponsor departed from the main company, and we are now working with the new controlling shareholders to restructure the business.

It is usually during times of distress that we realise that our interests are not (or are no longer) aligned with the sponsors, or that we can no longer trust them. For example, a CEO may sell company assets to pay back selected debt where he or she provided a personal guarantee, not recognising or acknowledging the order or priorities for all debts that must be serviced. They may have the company borrow more money and use the proceeds to buy a personal asset to service their personal debt. These sponsors are, effectively, putting their personal interests ahead of those of the business and shareholders.

In another example, in 2007, we were investors in a large taxi company. They made most of their profit not by transporting passengers around town, but by selling the used cars, the depreciated assets, after five years. These cars could typically be sold for around $5,000 in the second-hand market. The management of this company had also invested a lot of money – both personal and company – in real estate. In 2007 and 2008, interest rates went up, and suddenly loan payments were higher.

Managers at the company set up a new company, to which the main company would sell the used vehicles for $2,000, which would then in turn sell the vehicles on the market for $5,000. That amounted to a sizeable profit on each vehicle, which certainly came in handy to service personal debt at a time when interest rates were headed higher. However, the liabilities taken on by the company also ballooned as interest rates climbed, and the company became insolvent.

Then there was a coffee company which would buy beans from farmers, dry them, and then sell them to coffee buyers. They took a loan from a large private bank in Vietnam to fund working capital, with the coffee beans as collateral.

The dried coffee beans were meant to be stored in a silo, awaiting distribution. At some point, a representative of the bank went to visit the silo and guess what – it was empty. The management had stolen from the business, and the bank was left high and dry.

The takeaways

- As previously mentioned, we typically try to avoid control deals. We have only done a handful of them in over 100-plus deals for good reason: they are enormously challenging from a change-of-leadership perspective. In Vietnam, it is extremely difficult to find good executives to run your companies. The local pool is very shallow, which means we usually have to import an expat, which is expensive and more than likely won't work out as planned. The existing team tends to have an allergic reaction to the outsider. That results in a bypassing problem, where the long-time staff will go around the new CEO directly to the chairman. This usually results in the new CEO leaving in short order.

- As such, pursuing a minority investment strategy really means we must trust the management team and/or sponsor. Keep in mind, trust can erode over time, as business stress occurs, or hubris takes over as a result of success. In difficult times, one can really see how business leaders think and whose business interests they look after. And when times are good, leaders can become overconfident in their decisions and be less open to different points of view or ideas. Both scenarios will normally show investors whether management or the sponsor can be trusted.

• Find a business that has proven itself and achieved some level of success. Those qualities are usually associated with good, trusted management. Once you find and invest in them, back the management team and clearly define what you expect in terms of performance, and trust them to carry it out. If you have doubts about the capabilities of the management team of a potential investee, it is probably best to walk away.

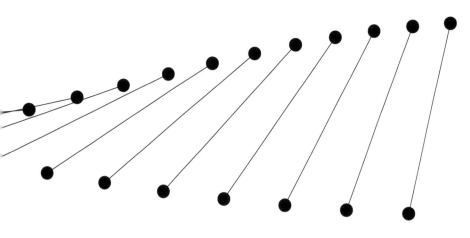

CHAPTER 4

THE 'NEVERS'

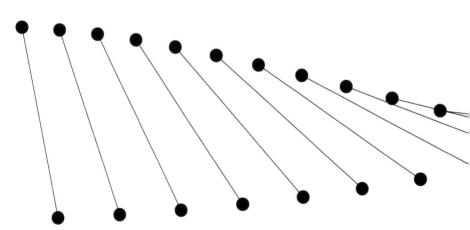

Each year, we typically have a pipeline of hundreds of potential investment opportunities we evaluate. Some sound interesting when they first come to our attention, but then we rule them out because they fail to meet two of our fundamental rules: alignment of interests and the ability to trust the management team to execute. We also have a host of 'nevers', which help us to further narrow the field of companies in which we might invest. Although these are not as black and white as the word 'never' might suggest, they do provide a good rule of thumb as we consider possible opportunities.

Rule 4: Never invest in a subsidiary

From time to time, we have been asked if we would be interested in investing in a subsidiary of a larger company, typically a Vietnam subsidiary of a foreign multinational. There may be any number of reasons why shares are being sold in the subsidiary, including general capital raising or preparation for an eventual spin-off. But most of the time in Vietnam, it is not so straightforward. We tend to steer clear of such investments (notwithstanding the example in the previous chapter), because generally speaking, it is tough to gauge the alignment of interests.

Subsidiaries may be established for purposes of managing taxes, transferring profits to the main company (the holding company, or holdco), where tax expenses may be minimised. There is nothing inherently wrong with that from a legal standpoint, but such arrangements will likely limit the growth of the subsidiary. More importantly, a number of conflicts of interest could arise, particularly around the issue of transfer pricing. For example, how will the subsidiary be charged for the implementation of a new IT system across the enterprise or compensated for land provided for the construction of a new factory? Assets can easily be diverted from the subsidiary. In developed markets, there are rules and regulations around how such things can be done in acceptable ways, but in Vietnam, those guidelines aren't usually followed – which could end up being disadvantageous to shareholders of the subsidiary.

Then there is the issue of resource allocation, both in terms of management's time and attention, as well as capital. If a holdco has a number of subsidiaries, where is the CEO devoting his or her attention (ideally, that attention should be focused on running the holdco)? Are the people running the subsidiaries good, and are their interests aligned with you as a shareholder in that business? Perhaps not, as the subsidiary will likely be closely aligned with the holdco's interests, leaving investors in the subsidiary as shareholders of a non-profit-optimised entity. Will the holdco sufficiently invest in the growth of the subsidiary so that you, as its prospective shareholder, will benefit to the fullest extent? That's not always clear.

The genesis of this rule goes back to 2005, before I joined VinaCapital. The company invested in a large food manufacturer located in HCMC. Shortly thereafter, the food maker set up a subsidiary in the north, a not uncommon move given the size of the country. However, in this case, the northern subsidiary had shareholders other than the main company in the south, and it evolved into an independent company. It even listed on the Ho Chi Minh Stock Exchange alongside its 'parent'.

It quickly became apparent that this relationship created conflicts of interest resulting in situations where shareholders in one company would not benefit from positive developments at the other. Management of the holdco was distracted, both by the northern subsidiary as well as another subsidiary it operated. And it had some issues around transfer pricing. Both companies traded at single-digit P/E ratios while the market's average P/E ratio was in the mid-teens, a clear sign that stockholders were not all that impressed by either company's management or performance.

Eventually, we worked with holdco management to bring the disparate subsidiaries back into the fold, and today it trades at a P/E ratio of 15–20×. This company is now one of Vietnam's top food manufacturers which, through various transactions and restructuring over the years, has created enormous value for its shareholders, including VinaCapital.

Vingroup (VIC) is Vietnam's largest conglomerate, with interests across many sectors, from residential property to shopping malls, hotels and resorts, to education and healthcare, as well as smartphones and Vietnam's only home-grown car brand, VinFast. The conglomerate model is often found in the early stages of South East Asian countries' development, and they have proven to be quite successful as they leverage important networks and relationships, and build scale.

VIC is an enormously successful enterprise that has made its founder Vietnam's wealthiest individual. It has also successfully listed two of its subsidiaries, Vinhomes (VHM), the residential property developer, and Vincom Retail (VRE), the operator of more than 70 shopping centres in Vietnam.

Would I make an exception to the rule in the case of VIC's subsidiaries? The answer is: it depends.

Not that long ago, VOF invested in VHM. Since it is a listed company, there is less potential information asymmetry as regulations require a range of disclosures, and in this case, after its initial public offering, it attracted large institutional investors such as KKR, GIC and Temasek. It has a largely independent board and has essentially evolved into a standalone entity. And since it is listed and liquid, we can sell our holdings whenever we see fit to do so.

The other listed subsidiary, VRE, is not of interest at this time. That's because it appears to be highly dependent on both its parent and VHM in terms of property, rental rates in the shopping centres it operates and other factors.

As for investing in the holdco itself, I generally prefer investing in companies that are focused, and VIC is involved in too many disparate sectors for my liking. As conglomerates are successful and grow, they can become increasingly complex in terms of finances and operations, and we are not smart enough to fully comprehend the potential conflicts of interest and misalignment of information given the many varied areas conglomerates are involved in.

Take, for example, the car company VinFast. It is owned not just by holdco, but also a separate investment company owned by its chairman,[3] which holds nearly 41%. With a capital investment of $4bn, VinFast became operational in a record amount of time. It took approximately 18 months between breaking ground on the new 355-hectare

---

3 "VinFast hikes charter capital by 37 pct", *VnExpress*, April 17, 2021.

state-of-the-art factory and turning on the robotic assembly lines and building cars – a truly amazing achievement! But a shareholder of VIC might have concerns about the potential for conflicts of interest down the road.

While VIC is a credible and well-known company – and any such concerns are likely unwarranted – there are many more small and less sophisticated private companies that may have management who are not as transparent about these kinds of issues. I prefer to avoid opportunities for potential conflict right from the start.

All of that said, had one invested in VIC at the time of its listing in September 2007 and held to 31 March 2021, one would have enjoyed an annual return of 22.6%. But the success of VIC has not been replicated at the listed subsidiaries. Had one invested at the time of listing for VRE (November 2017) and VHM (May 2018) and held to the end of March 2021, one would have broken even for VRE and made a small 2% return for VHM. These returns reinforce my belief that investments in subsidiaries are usually best avoided.

In 2014, there was another local company that was very successful in its 'day job' of acting as a wholesaler for a number of well-known international consumer brands, as well as operating restaurants. It was the largest such company in Vietnam at that time. The CEO transferred much of the wholesale business to a newly formed subsidiary, and a large Japanese private-equity fund subsequently invested in the subsidiary. The 'main' company was to refocus on building a distribution network for Japanese brands interested in entering the Vietnam market. While I haven't really kept track of the company, in recent times it is understood that the fund was interested in selling its stake in the subsidiary; perhaps unsurprisingly, there has been little interest from buyers. There would be a high likelihood of conflicts of interest and questions about resource allocation.

We have also seen occasions where a multinational corporation has tried to spin off its local operating subsidiary. Again, in this instance we ultimately feel that as good as the operation might be, it is beholden to the holdco first and foremost, for better or worse.

Now, for a major exception to the rule: SOEs. It is often possible to invest in the subsidiaries of SOEs via the equitisation or privatisation process. Why would these scenarios be interesting, especially given the added complication of government involvement?

Actually, these opportunities tend to tick all the right boxes. First, the companies are usually quite transparent – there are no transfer pricing issues given that state assets are involved and the potential penalties for playing games are significant, such as jail time. Second, management's interest is aligned with shareholders because they typically participate in the equitisation of the subsidiary.

Vietnam Rubber Group is one such example. As the name suggests, its primary business is the production of rubber. It is owned almost entirely by the government. But it also has several subsidiaries, including one that owns land (primarily tapped-out rubber plantations) and is developing industrial parks to meet the accelerating demand for manufacturing space in Vietnam. This is one case where we would consider investing in a subsidiary.

The issues around investing in subsidiaries are not limited to Vietnam – they are global. However, the pitfalls that tend to come with these kinds of investments – capital resources, leadership focus, conflicts of interest – are probably more prevalent here. And the opportunities to remedy problems in the legal system remain limited.

The takeaway

- Investments in subsidiaries rarely allow for a proper alignment of interests and create situations of information asymmetry. It is usually best to avoid them.

Rule 5: Never build a greenfield hotel...

The hospitality sector has long been of interest to VinaCapital, and over the years the way we invest in the sector has evolved.

In the early 2000s, Vietnam's tourism sector started to open up. Existing hotels operators – mostly state-owned companies like Hanoi Tourist and Saigon Tourist – sought to upgrade their properties, while international operators looked for local partners to enable them to enter Vietnam for the first time. That led to a building boom in many parts of the country, particularly in scenic coastal cities such as Nha Trang and Danang in central Vietnam. At one point, VinaCapital and VOF had ownership interests in eight hotels in Vietnam, from north to south, including the Metropole Hotel in Hanoi and the Sheraton Nha Trang.

Case study: Sheraton Nha Trang – The primary reason behind this rule

Source: Sheraton Nha Trang

In December 2006, VinaCapital was asked to take over a project to build a three-star hotel overlooking the picturesque seven-kilometre white-sand beach of Nha Trang. The original budget estimate for the project: $34m.

Nha Trang was already a relatively well-known resort town, and the local airport was in the process of being migrated to a former US airbase on the outskirts of town and which could handle international flights. Nha Trang and its immediate surroundings were long popular with a wide range of tourists, especially those from the former Soviet Union. More than 5.8 million international tourists visited Vietnam in 2006, and the projections were for the number of inbound visitors to rise sharply, so investing in a mid-range hospitality project seemed like a good idea. (Those forecasts proved reasonably accurate: in 2019, more than 18 million people visited Vietnam.)

I hadn't yet joined VinaCapital, but my understanding is that at some point, the decision was taken to convert the 28-floor project to a five-star resort, to be managed by an international hotel chain. Given the growing numbers of foreign tourists, especially from Europe and North America, this was probably a key consideration – to build a property of the standards such tourists might expect (and be willing to pay for). This made sense to us.

In July 2007, VinaCapital signed a 15-year hotel management agreement with Starwood Hotels, which owned the Sheraton brand. At this stage, construction was not yet complete, and the hotel was expected to open some 18 months later in January 2009. International hotel companies have a wide variety of requirements for the hotels they manage to fit the brand and image they aim to convey. This ranges from the colour of the carpets and wallpaper, to the style of furnishings and the brands of mattresses, as well as the available amenities and services. For this project, the requisite upgrades were not cheap – to be expected when taking a locally run three-star property and transforming it to an international-standard five-star one – the budget estimate mushroomed to over $51m.

What happened next was a perfect storm of price increases and cost overruns that required the project be refinanced several times. The shareholders (i.e., VinaCapital) had to provide an emergency loan (at a time when the lending rates of Vietnamese banks was 20%) to ensure the project met its legal capital requirements.

Inflation skyrocketed in 2008, peaking at an all-time high of 28% in August that year. At year's end, the 2008 inflation rate was an incredible 23.12%. Construction costs soared by 33% between Q4 2007 and Q1 2008, in part due to a 25% increase in the price of concrete.

In addition to the price increases and cost overruns, a regulatory issue suddenly cropped up. It seemed that the hotel's rotating viewing tower caused an 'encroachment of air space' and the local authorities required the hotel to obtain additional land-use rights to account for the overhang.

In an email to investors, the project manager listed the construction cost blowouts as line items. Some of the notable overruns included a 129% increase in the cost of sanitary fixtures and fittings, a 143% increase in the cost of ceiling finishes, a 185% increase in the cost of graphics and signage, a 77% increase in the cost of painting, and a 101% increase in the cost of exterior work. Cost controls were clearly not a high consideration back then.

The email went on to disclose that the original estimate of construction costs in 2007 was $28.1m. A year later, the estimate had increased nearly 40% to $38.8m. At the end of the day, the costs reached $63.5m due to drastic increases in construction, building materials and higher-quality equipment.

Of course, members of the investment committee expressed strong concerns about the ballooning costs. They also questioned the hotel's projected returns, given that it was in a resort town with seasonal fluctuations in tourism, and ours was not the only international-brand property under construction – the Intercontinental Nha Trang was being built directly next door and other hotels were going up around town.

The hotel finally opened in March 2010, more than a year behind schedule. But occupancy rates were lower than expected, in part due to the increased competition in the Nha Trang tourism market, which also put downward pressure on room rates. By the end of that year, the occupancy rate was 22%, compared to the predicted 36%, and the average room rate was 30% less than we had projected, at $102 per night.

VinaCapital sold most of its stake in 2013 but continues to have a minority interest in the property. Fortunately, the Sheraton Nha Trang found its stride just as tourism in Vietnam took off. But it took a while, and the experience was enough to teach us a very hard lesson.

Case study: The Metropole Hanoi – A case where things worked out well

Source: Lodgis Hospitality Holdings

The Metropole Hotel is a beautiful colonial-era hotel located in the French quarter of downtown Hanoi, between the popular tourist sites of the Opera House and Hoan Kiem Lake. It has long been considered the 'grand dame' of the city's historic hotel. Originally called the Grand Hotel Metropole, it opened in 1901, and hosted a procession of celebrities. Charlie Chaplin honeymooned there in 1936 after marrying Hollywood starlet Paulette Goddard. British novelist Somerset Maugham stayed at the hotel to complete his novel, *The Gentleman In The Parlour*, an account of his journey through Myanmar, Thailand, Cambodia and Vietnam (then known as Burma, Siam and Indochina) in 1923.

More recently, during the Vietnam-America war, noted anti-war activists Joan Baez, the singer, and actress Jane Fonda stayed at the Metropole, and both spent time in the hotel's bomb shelter. Pre- and post-war, it has been the hotel of choice for visiting diplomats and heads of state.

VinaCapital invested in the Metropole Hotel in September 2005, initially paying $10m for a 28.8% stake in what was then a 232-room hotel with offices and retail space. State-run Hanoi Tourist owned 50%, with smaller shareholders owning the remainder. The valuation of the hotel was about $60m.

By the time we bought our stake, the hotel had seen better days and was in need of a massive renovation to bring it back to its former glory. Once spruced up, we believed the hotel could potentially attract a more diverse clientele, including domestic travellers, who tend to be the biggest spenders in Vietnamese hotels.

As a five-star international hotel, the Metropole is relatively low-rise – only seven storey high – even though it sits on 7,469 square metres. The local government was committed to maintaining the site in its current form – it would not allow it to be demolished so that a modern skyscraper could be built. We set out to refurbish the property from top to bottom in stages, converting the office space to 130 more hotel rooms, increasing the total to 364 rooms, a rise of 50%. Unlike in Nha Trang, the hotel was operational, so the hotel's profits were used to fund the renovation and there was no requirement to inject further capital into the project. Furthermore, the costs were very predictable, as they were working to a template, i.e., the existing parts of the hotel.

In 2011, during renovations of the hotel's Bamboo Bar, the historic wartime bunkers were rediscovered after being forgotten for more than 40 years. The musty rooms are now one of Hanoi's most popular tourist sites, with the hotel offering 'Path of History' tours through them.

Over the course of our investment, we increased our stake to 50%. The Metropole became a 'trophy asset' for VinaCapital and VOF, a profitable, one-of-a-kind business that would be very attractive to investors. In 2016, 11 years after buying into the Metropole, VOF sold its 50% stake in the hotel for $104m.

The takeaway

- New builds are rife with opportunities for costs to spiral out of control, especially if the property is to be operated under an international brand. Hotel owners are typically subject to the specifications and standards required by multinational hotel operators. In our experience, building new hotels or undertaking major refurbishments to upgrade a property from a three-star to a five-star resort can lead to major cost overruns. It is better to invest in operating properties with histories and reputations.

Rule 6: ...or build a hospital

Healthcare is one of those sectors in Vietnam that has seen immense improvement over the past two decades. The public health system is expansive, with major general and specialty hospitals in the larger cities, and a network of smaller hospitals and clinics in second-tier cities, towns, and villages. But like most public health systems, it is overburdened, understaffed and underfunded. This created an opportunity for private hospitals, which were first legally recognised in the late 1990s.

In September 2009, VinaCapital was approached by Dr Nguyen Huu Tung, a respected and experienced physician who established the Hoan My Group, a private hospital company. Founded in 1999, the Hoan My Group was built on the premise of providing high-quality and affordable healthcare with "the patient at the centre of every decision". Dr Tung was seeking investors to help his company fund the construction of a new hospital project in HCMC.

Hoan My Hospital Saigon

At the time, private medical facilities accounted for only 5% of Vietnam's 1,107 hospitals, and 2.9% of beds. The growing affluence of the population meant the pool of people seeking and willing to pay for better medical treatment was growing. Between 2000 and 2006, the compounded annual growth rate (CAGR) of the private healthcare sector was an impressive 33.6%.

Healthcare was a new sector for us, but we knew that the Hoan My Group was considered the top private healthcare provider in the country, with a well-known brand, a solid reputation for providing quality care, and a base of more than one million patients a year. It operated five hospitals across Vietnam, two in HCMC and then one each in Dalat, Danang, and Can Tho. The group employed more than 2,000 people, including 220 doctors and pharmacists, and 430 nurses and technicians. With a decade of experience, Hoan My offered a very interesting investment proposition amid very compelling growth trends for the sector.

The company's strong profit forecast for the next three years, and the knowledge that the land value for the hospitals in Danang and HCMC would cover the initial investment if the projected cash flow wasn't achieved, made the investment attractive. VinaCapital acquired 6.3 million shares for $10m, and alongside us, Deutsche Bank acquired convertible bonds equivalent to $10m.

The need for the investment came from the construction of Phan Xich Long Hospital in HCMC's Phu Nhuan District. It was planned as a 200-bed facility with an original budget of around $19m, including $9m for the building and $6.5m for equipment.

As construction progressed, VinaCapital discovered that the hospital equipment costs had been significantly underestimated. By July 2010, the budget had swollen by 57% to over $40m – the result of higher interest rates, high inflation, and rising building and equipment costs.

While the increases in interest rates and construction costs were external factors that couldn't really be predicted, the cost overruns on equipment were the result of poor design and poor planning. There is generally a three- to four-year lag between a hospital being designed and the construction being completed. In that time, some of the medical equipment in the original design can become obsolete, and whatever next-generation equipment a manufacturer sells will often have different specifications, requiring modifications to rooms, ventilation, wall surfaces, and so on.

For example, the hospital's original design included a 64-slice CT scanner. But when it came time to order the machine, it was no longer available. Instead, Hoan My had to buy the faster, more accurate, and much more expensive 128-slice CT scanner. This type of scanner cost almost double its predecessor, at around $1m. The hospital's original design also did not include any MRI scanning facilities, but a decision was made to include an MRI machine, which cost around $2m. These two machines alone accounted for half of the 74% increase in equipment costs between the original design and the final hospital project.

Another cost overrun was for the operating room equipment, in which the original plan used made-in-China equipment. But, as with the CT scanner, the equipment was no longer available, and the hospital needed to procure much more expensive equipment manufactured by Japan's Hitachi Healthcare.

While these ballooning costs at the new hospital were cause for serious concern and headaches, we ultimately invested in Hoan My Group as a company, not just that single hospital.

In 2011, VinaCapital sold its stake in Hoan My Group in two tranches, totalling $23.38m. Hoan My Group founder Dr Tung, who held a 55.2% stake, wanted to sell a controlling stake of his company to India-based Fortis Healthcare Global Pte, in a transaction that valued the company at $100m. Recognising that there was still some room for growth, we held on to a 5% stake, which we sold to the Richard Chandler Corporation one year later, when it purchased the company from Fortis. Despite the haemorrhaging costs at the Phan Xich Long Hospital project, our 20-month investment in Hoan My Group was a success.

In 2017, it was estimated that Vietnamese spend approximately $2bn on overseas medical care, evidence of both the rising affluence of the Vietnamese consumer and the continued potential for high-quality healthcare services at home. That is why the private healthcare sector is one where we continue to invest. In fact, VOF has assembled a portfolio of hospital companies across the country – including a stake in Dr Tung's successor company, Tam Tri Medical, which is the largest hospital platform of its kind.

Another hospital group in our portfolio is Thai Hoa, which operates two facilities in the Mekong Delta. When we bought into the group in 2016, Thai Hoa operated one hospital, with a second under construction. In this case, we applied the lessons we learned from Hoan My and went through the budget for the new facility with a fine-tooth comb. Furthermore, medical equipment purchases were not made until the end of the planning and design process. The new facility is almost identical to the original one; the exterior looks the same while the interior and floor plans are very similar. As a result, the construction of the new hospital – which opened in 2019 – actually came in *under* budget

The takeaway

- Invest in a healthcare group with established operations and reputations – new-build hospitals are to be avoided. Similar to building new hotels, cost overruns are common, but the root cause is related to design changes which accommodate newer, state-of-the-art equipment and machinery.

Rule 7: Avoid export businesses and body shops

We don't invest in export businesses. Now, I understand that might sound odd, being located in a country where exports have grown at an average rate of 17% from 2010–2020. But there are a couple of things to keep in mind.

First, many of those exports are being produced by FDI companies such as Samsung, LG, or Intel. Second, much of what is being exported is being produced under contract. Related to that point is the fact that these contract manufacturers are competing with companies domestically in the South East Asia region (in Thailand and Indonesia), and internationally with China. This kind of manufacturing is always a race to the bottom – the company that can produce the product at the lowest cost will win. Finally, these businesses are capital-intensive, and the cost of capital in Vietnam is high.

The three key elements of export businesses are:

1. **Labour**

2. **Input**

3. **Scale**

Looking at Vietnam, the low cost of **labour** is a prime, if not primary, consideration for manufacturers in Vietnam. Employee wages are about one-third to one-half of those in China.

Inputs are another story entirely. Most of the products manufactured in Vietnam require the importation of inputs, from semiconductors and LCD screens, to wood and cotton. Apart from some commodities (e.g., coffee, fruits and vegetables, seafood), there are not yet a whole lot of inputs produced here – the local supply chain is still to be developed. So, the costs and time associated with importing inputs can fluctuate based on a range of variables.

Scale, or producing more units of a product amortised against fixed costs, is important because if you don't have that, you lose to China. A company needs to build a massive operation to achieve scale. China is the main example of scale, but Thailand has also been successful in this regard, in one sector at least: automobile and parts production. Its Eastern Economic Corridor to the southeast of Bangkok is home to numerous auto-manufacturers and their suppliers. They have successfully achieved a scale whereby it is easier and cheaper to produce cars there and export throughout the region, including to Vietnam. (Thailand accounted for 38% of all new cars imported by Vietnam in the first eight months of 2020,[4] with Indonesia a close second at 32%.)

A manufacturer in Vietnam producing goods for export was probably chosen because it was cheap. This has certainly been a factor in the rapid development of the apparel and footwear sector, which is why most of the major shoemakers, like Nike and Adidas, and many clothing brands manufacture here. But at some point, labour costs may reach a level where notoriously thin margins in apparel are squeezed, and companies move production contracts to places like Cambodia or Bangladesh.

We have seen a similar dynamic in the furniture industry, where there are hundreds of contract manufacturers for the likes of Ikea, Costco and Home Depot, thanks to their low costs and good quality. But the margins are thin – it is a race to the bottom, as the customer is always focused on reducing costs.

So what about inputs – clearly Vietnam can compete on that basis, one might say. In reality, Vietnam does not produce anything particularly special. It is the world's second largest producer of the mineral tungsten, but there is very little value added in-country. There is some offshore oil drilling, but nearly all of it is refined at the country's one oil refinery and used domestically.

Vietnam is home to a range of agricultural and fisheries products, such as a range of fruits, coffee, cocoa, cashew nuts, prawns, and the pangasius/basa fish. But again, products see very little value added there. And we tend to steer clear of commodities due to their tendency for wild fluctuations. These

---

4 "Viet Nam imported 53,000 CBU cars in 8 months", *Vietnam News Biz Hub*, 9 September 2020.

raw materials are simply grown, produced, or extracted, and then exported. There's not a lot of conversion happening here.

Steel is one material that is increasingly being exported to the world from Vietnam. But a few years ago, the country's steelmakers (including Hoa Phat Group, the biggest company and a long-time holding in VOF's portfolio) had to start importing iron ore to meet growing demand.

In theory, a company could produce coconut water for export. Coconuts are abundant in Vietnam, especially in the Mekong Delta. But reaching a scale and quality suitable for export would take a sizeable investment, and that company would be competing with brands from other countries such as Thailand, Indonesia, or Malaysia, where coconuts are also abundant. The margins are likely to be compressed.

One final issue with export businesses is that they require enormous amounts of working capital – they essentially serve as a bank to their customers.

They likely have to import the raw materials they need to produce the goods they sold. They pay for those raw materials, which are then shipped. It could be days or weeks before they arrive, and it may sit in storage. The conversion takes place, accruing labour costs. The finished goods are then shipped, with fees paid to all of the logistics providers. Then it may take weeks to ship the products to the US or Europe. And finally, on arrival, the customer will receive the products – and then pay the manufacturer on 30-, 60- or even 90-day terms!

Consider all of those working capital costs, and then consider the cost of capital. Foreign companies have a low cost of capital. For Vietnamese companies, the cost of borrowing is between

6% and 10%, and there are no fixed-interest-rate loans in Vietnam, be it for businesses or mortgages – they are adjusted every 3–6 months. Maintaining the necessary working capital is a very expensive proposition.

Of course, larger, more mature businesses are equipped to handle this dynamic more efficiently. They also tend to be the exception to the rule. We would consider investing in companies with established brands in their home market looking to export. One example is Vinamilk (another long-time holding), which now exports its milk to a range of markets around the world, such as the Middle East, Cambodia, and the Philippines. But Vinamilk only started exporting after it had reached a saturation point in Vietnam, where it commands 79% market share for condensed milk and 59% for liquid milk (and more than 80% in yoghurt). It built and polished its brand here before looking to export. At present, exports account for less than a quarter of its sales.

There is also a coffee brand, Trung Nguyen Coffee, which has cafes across the country and in a few overseas markets. They have built a strong reputation for their various roasts and flavours, and now export to more than 60 countries around the world, primarily under its own brand. There is more about this interesting company in a later chapter.

The commonalities between Vinamilk and Trung Nguyen Coffee are: both companies did well in their home market before exporting, and both have built consumer-facing brands with value. Their brand value contributes to their products' value. Conversely, a contract manufacturing furniture company in Binh Duong province is unknown to consumers because they pursued an original equipment manufacturer (OEM) model rather than developing their own retail brand.

The rule to avoid export businesses stems from a fairly early investment the fund made back in 2007. There was a furniture company that was booming due to its large sales to major Western hotel operators. We thought we had found a brand that could potentially appeal directly to consumers.

Companies like Marriott would order thousands of nightstands and armoires from this company at a time; the volume was good, but the margins were not. They would have to bid on one project after another, with cost the key factor as to whether they won an order or not. We exited our investment in this company in 2010 at cost. The company still operates today, although it has been experiencing difficulties for several years.

The important lesson was that business-to-business companies that engage in contract manufacturing are vulnerable to the various uncontrollable market forces and must focus on the costs of their customers.

As Vietnam moves up the value chain and is able to manufacture higher-value products and those that require greater intellectual knowledge, a different situation could emerge whereby a company producing primarily for export might be interesting to us. But even things like semiconductors and cars can be copied and ultimately reduced to costs.

Body shops are another kind of business that we will pass on. I'm not referring to the shop that will knock the dent out of your car's fender, but rather professional service firms and investment companies where people are the primary assets. These businesses continually require more people to grow revenue. There are two key issues with body shops:

1. **They don't scale.** A scalable business can grow its gross margin, squeezing out more income from each unit. In body shops, the unit is a person, and there is only so much one person can produce.

2. **People can walk.** Good employees can hold the business hostage to their demands. They will want higher wages, or they may want to be a partner in the business. If they are not happy with what they are given, they can ultimately walk out the door, often with their clients. The most valuable assets a business has can hold it hostage.

Some may say that higher compensation expenses at body shops can be mitigated by raising the prices for customers. But markets, particularly developing ones like Vietnam, can only absorb so much. The partners of the Vietnam offices of some of the big-name Western law firms can command hourly rates close (if not equal) to their peers back home. That's because their expertise cannot easily be replaced, and their counsel is valued. However, there are only so many situations that warrant such high-powered counsel, and only a handful of companies operating here that can afford those rates. For more standard, straightforward legal work, companies will turn to smaller local firms where the counsel is good and the costs more affordable.

In Vietnam, the talent pool of experienced professionals is still relatively shallow. I mentioned earlier how difficult it is to find good CEOs, and the same holds true for attorneys, accountants, and others.

Typically, in a country that is developing, the professional class is made up of foreigners and locals who had the chance to study and work overseas. Then, as multinational firms set up in a country, locals will work there and gain valuable experience in how things should be done. After a period of time, some of those locals who worked for the multinationals will be recruited by local companies looking to step up their game, or the employee will start his or her own company in a related business. This is a pattern that has been seen in China, and I would expect it to happen in Vietnam, too. However, it may take a while, as multinationals have not operated in Vietnam for all that long yet.

Another business I could classify as a body shop is hospitals. In many cases, hospitals in Vietnam become well known because of the reputation of an individual physician, or a small group of physicians. If they are not part of the hospital's ownership, they could threaten to go elsewhere. That is exactly what we have seen with a group that specialises in in-vitro fertilisation (IVF). They practise at a leading hospital and they are always in demand. To placate their talent, the hospital's management has limited expanding the practice (i.e., they can't scale it up) and they always have to deal with the potential that at some point, these doctors might be made an offer from someone else that they just cannot refuse.

Now, if you are familiar with the fund I manage (or have read my previous rule), you are probably saying to yourself, "wait a minute – aren't you one of the biggest investors in private healthcare in Vietnam?" We are indeed. But the key to our approach is investing in healthcare systems comprised of many doctors and many locations. They may not be particularly well known as individuals, but they are good, and the facilities are known to provide quality care. We are less at risk of being compromised by the whims of star players. Nevertheless, hospitals are required to take on more staff to scale up, but in this case, there are many other factors at play that make these investments attractive.

The takeaway

- Export businesses have high working capital needs, and their margins are continually under pressure. Body shops are difficult and expensive to scale up and operate, and can potentially be held hostage by their biggest assets – their people! Both are best avoided.

Rule 8: Never buy anything from another 'healthy' fund or financial investor

From time to time, another fund or financial investor will quietly sound us out about our interest in buying an asset from their private-equity portfolio. The first question that always comes to mind is this: if the asset is so good, why do they want to sell it?

The chances are, it is not as good as it looks.

Fund managers are all pretty much alike. We have the same DNA, we think similarly, and we think we are smarter than everyone else. If we see the manager of a healthy fund shopping a private-equity stake or selling out, we know there is nothing for us to buy. Because if we all think alike, then we know that they are selling because something is wrong at that business or they are trying to get an unjustifiable valuation.

What we have found is there is usually an information asymmetry. The seller knows something about their investment that may – or may not – be discovered as part of due diligence, or that there is an issue quietly fermenting, waiting to explode at some point in the future.

The point is, if the asset being sold by the fund is so successful, why aren't they pursuing the more traditional ways of exiting, such as a listing on the stock exchange or a strategic sale?

A related issue is buying something from a fund that is *not* healthy. Occasionally there have been funds that have wound down their operations for any number of reasons; they may have never gotten traction in the market or succeeded in fundraising, or experienced turmoil in the ranks of their managers. Whatever the cause, they will typically seek to sell their holdings as a package.

For example, a few years back, VinaCapital (not VOF) purchased a range of holdings from a venture capital fund in Vietnam that was shutting its doors. The seller (who was very familiar to us) allowed us to purchase these assets at a very reasonable valuation. There were some promising companies in the portfolio and some not so promising. As is typical in venture capital, not all of the investments panned out, but we were ultimately able to make the overall investment work.

Another example is a limited partner (LP) or general partner (GP) fund approaching the end of its life and, as a result, it has to liquidate a number of positions in its portfolio. One of its holdings is a 10% stake in a privately held chemical company. The fund manager is asking an unjustifiably high price for its stake. Furthermore, they did not seek a commitment from their sponsor to list. As a result, this fund is finding it extremely difficult to find a buyer. Why?

Few investors are going to be interested in paying such an expensive price for an illiquid stock that comes with no rights or protections. And since the buyer is buying from the fund – essentially a vendor – and not the sponsor, it is unlikely that the buyer would even have the opportunity to negotiate rights with the sponsor. Fund managers tend to be aggressive in the valuations of their stakes, but buying at a high price and having no terms in a private position is not attractive at all to me.

The takeaway

- Healthy private-equity funds are selling a business because there's something wrong – there's nothing to see and best to move along.

Rule 9: Never invest in a company belonging to your friend... or your enemy

Doing business with friends or family is rarely a good idea. It is very likely that the issues that tend to arise in business will negatively affect the relationship. Unfortunately, when you work at an investment company, the chance that you will be asked for help is high.

The request typically starts off innocent enough. They will not immediately ask for your money but your advice. They know you do deals and now want to tap your experience so they can raise capital and expand their business. You will tell them about what banks look for when making loans (i.e., collateral and cash flow) or what external investors usually ask for in return for their investment (terms). They may also want to know how to properly value their company. Essentially, you have to school them on finance and investing. It may take some time but is otherwise fine. If they are somehow successful in obtaining financing, you're done, case closed.

But what usually happens is that they aren't successful in obtaining a bank loan or enticing a third party to invest, and they have exhausted their options. That's usually because their business is not as interesting as they think it is (and you don't have the guts to tell them so), or the bank did not think there was enough collateral put up for the loan amount, or it's an uninteresting proposition to a third-party investor for some other reason. Lo and behold, your friend or family member asks you to invest, and now you are in a bind. Should you invest?

Because the person asking you to invest is a close friend, you consider it, even though you know that if you proceed, you are creating a series of strains on the relationship. Where do you start? The first pothole on this road is valuing your friend's business. If you do it yourself, you risk your friend thinking you low-balled the valuation, so instead you suggest hiring a banker or some other external party to come up with the valuation. These services cost money – who is going to pay for that?

Then you have to explain topics like the cost of equity, the cost of debt, multiples, terms and conditions, penalties, and a range of other subjects related to investing. What started out as providing helpful advice quickly turns to an experience akin to going to the dentist.

If neither side has given up after that, you get down to explaining the commitments (revenue, profit after tax, or EBITDA, annualised or the average of three years) and the fact that you expect 15–25% growth. You mention things like governance (which they probably don't have), penalties, and so on – all of the terms and conditions you typically negotiate with your arm's-length investees.

The real difficulty comes around the penalties for not meeting the commitments – that's where things get tough. If you end up needing to exercise the penalties (and let's be honest: it's likely you will), your friendship is probably over. What for you is a rational business transaction is not the same for your friend, who is emotionally invested in their business and will perceive your actions on a personal level.

Nine out of ten of the companies we invest in have something go wrong over the course of the investment. That's ok, as most of the problems can be rectified one way or the other, but that's business. With a friend (and especially with a family member), business problems may force skeletons out of the closet. They are not likely to take kindly to that, and the relationship will be strained.

Let's say that your friend's company actually performed well enough that you as a financial investor are ready to exit. That's another area of strain. For us, an exit is not emotional – remember that we invest with a three- to five-year horizon and we will need to exit when we think the timing is right to generate the best return. But for the founder, your exit may be viewed on a personal level.

Another strain is the indirect pressure these investments can cause. The economic relationship gets pushed to the side by emotions. If you invested in your brother's business and you have been tough with him, he may get the parents or other siblings involved. Or if you invest in your friend's business, where his wife is the diligent CFO, and they get divorced, whose side are you on? Your cheating friend the husband, or the wife who knows how to run the business? This dynamic is even worse when the divorcing couple are family.

If you think the relationship dynamics were awkward and uncomfortable pre-investment, it's possible they will get even worse post-investment. The situation is rife with opportunities for misunderstandings and conflict, especially if you discover there has been leakage in the business. You, as the financier, become the bad person. You hold the money; you call the terms.

Part of the genesis of this rule relates to a situation where we were approached by a friend from Hanoi who owned a successful entertainment and F&B company. Seeking to expand her business, she approached banks about a loan. They scoffed, rightfully noting that the business actually had very few assets – all of the spaces were rented, and inventory was relatively small. Next, she came to me and a few other friends and asked whether we would invest in her business. Instead, we provided a loan with a sweetheart interest rate.

In making the loan, we required governance changes – she had no real board, and those she did have didn't meet often; there were no KPIs; no minutes – as well as the hiring of a proper CFO. She used a bookkeeper, and there was no analysis of budgets or cost controls – she would insist on premium furnishings and fixtures in her establishments. Surprisingly, there was no one responsible for marketing for the entire group of venues, although some individual restaurants and clubs had a marketing person.

It should be noted that the friend was very good at one part of the business. She was very successful at creating clubs that appealed to people who like to spend a lot on bottle service and show off; places where young people could drive up in their Ferraris and have a valet park their car in a prominent location out the front, and order expensive bottles of whisky or champagne (which boast profit margins of about 80%) for themselves and their friends. Casual-dining restaurants, on the other hand, are a completely different ballgame. Customers want good food and service in clean establishments; margins in the restaurant business are notoriously low.

Over time, we figured out that she was unlikely to improve governance or any of the other problem areas we had identified. We ended up taking equity in the business to pay off the loan. Ultimately, she was successful in attracting some high-profile individuals to invest and we got our money back.

The lesson is that if you are inclined to support the business of a friend or family member, the best option is probably a loan that is clear on the interest rate, repayment date, and the collateral, which could include personal assets, such as shares in the business (but be prepared to kick them out of the business), cars, or homes. But make sure the home pledged is a second home – if they only have one home, don't touch it. You don't want to find yourself in a position where you have to kick them out!

Investing in an enemy

One might ask why someone would ever consider investing in the companies of their enemies. Well, revenge is a very strong emotion for some people. You can't achieve that with a minority stake – you need to take a controlling stake and sit on the board if you want to give your enemy a hard time or get them out. And you always have to be wary that your enemy may still be able to hurt you. Emotion is never a good motivation for investing.

We were once presented with the chance to invest in a project run by a nemesis, but quickly dismissed it. It wasn't worth it.

In fact, we are probably more likely to *help* an enemy in some way, even if we do not invest, with the hope that they will not remain an enemy forever. Again, looking at situations objectively, with as little emotion as possible, is the right way to invest.

The takeaways

- Investing in the businesses of friends or family members is rarely worth the trouble it is likely to cause to the relationships. It also creates enormous conflicts of interest. And forget about investing in the business of enemies – whatever initial satisfaction you may get is likely to end up going horribly wrong.

- If you are inclined to help a family member or friend with their business, providing a loan is a much more straightforward solution.

Rule 10: No money out!

When we invest in a business, we expect our money to be used to contribute to its growth, not go into the pocket of the owner. 'Money in' refers to when we make our investment and it goes directly into the business, whereas 'money out' means that our investment is paid to a shareholder or sponsor. When investing via listed stocks, that's very straightforward and considered money out. But in private equity in Vietnam, you have to be wary of money out. In the case of money out, cash being paid to the sponsor for the company's shares may then be used in other areas, leading the sponsor to defocus on the targeted business.

It is understandable that a founder, who may have spent all or most of their life building a business, wants to take some money out to secure the future of his family. He may buy a house or provide his kids with a good education. Within reason, we have no issue with that. We want the founder to be focused on continuing to grow the business. He needs to continue to be a major shareholder with most of his wealth tied to the business.

However, if we see a lot of money out, we have reason to be concerned. There could be one of two issues at play. First, it could be a matter of asymmetric information. There could be something wrong in the business, such as an imminent contingent liability of which you were not informed, or perhaps he knows the business has peaked. Second, the founder, suddenly flush with cash, might have become defocused.

In Vietnam, it is not uncommon to see a male founder or CEO become defocused when he suddenly has newfound wealth. With too much cash in hand, we often see them:

1. **Invest in real estate.** Property is perhaps the favourite asset for Vietnamese people to invest in.

2. **Gamble.** This is another popular activity in this part of the world.

3. **Provide for mistress(es).** Having a mistress is a fairly common occurrence in Vietnam, whether condoned or not.

4. **Play more golf.** This hobby is popular among the newly rich, who can now afford the equipment and green fees at courses around the country.

Each of these is troubling in their own way, not necessarily from a moral perspective, but rather from the potential risks we have seen them cause the businesses they own and/or manage and in which we invest.

For example, real estate in and of itself is not an issue – it has proven to be a very good investment in Vietnam. But many people will overleverage to buy prime properties that they think they can sell or develop in a few years' time and thus, unnecessarily subject themselves to market risks. Oftentimes, they will use the company's credit score or property, or their own shares in the company as collateral to secure personal loans to buy property.

If things go wrong with a property investment – and they frequently do – the collateral will be put under pressure. We have witnessed several instances where a sponsor used company cash to buy treasury shares in an effort to maintain or prop up share prices so they could avoid margin calls. Clearly, this puts the sponsor in a conflict-of-interest situation relative to the company's shareholders.

Vietnamese people are not legally allowed to gamble in the country's few casinos (although the government is running a trial at two casinos), but that has not stopped them from gambling in more *informal* ways or, pre-Covid-19, from traveling to Cambodia, Singapore or Macao to play the tables. If an individual is charged and convicted of gambling in Vietnam, under the law they are prohibited from serving as an officer or board member of a company, notwithstanding the reputational issues caused to the company.

A newly wealthy founder may have taken up with a mistress, perhaps someone he met at nightclub as he was splashing out for bottle service. An extramarital affair is certainly a personal matter, but it can quickly spiral into a business matter. Properly maintaining a mistress with an apartment, clothes, and/or car is an expensive proposition totalling about $5,000 per month (or so I'm told). And beyond the money, the affair can lead to marital strife and flaring of emotions. It can be expensive in more ways than one!

Finally, there's golf. The sport is quite expensive in Vietnam, a pastime for wealthy Vietnamese people, expats, and tourists. What's even worse is when someone bets on golf. In all seriousness, the occasional round of golf can be good for business networking and an outlet to relieve stress. But if a founder or CEO of a company in which I have invested tells me how much he has improved his handicap, I will consider exiting the investment. Practising golf takes a lot of time and money, and to me is a clear signal that the individual is losing focus on his business.

In contrast to their male counterparts, female founders and CEOs tend to remain focused. Although they may dabble in real estate, they usually have a better ability to negotiate good deals. They are much less likely to gamble, and the only reason they tend to play golf is for the business that might occur on the course. As for affairs, they tend to be much more discreet. Admittedly these are broad generalisations, but accurate from my experience. We have generally had fewer issues with our investee companies led by women.

A case where money out signalled something was wrong with the business

A few years ago, we invested in a company that built infrastructure in exchange for land. The need for new infrastructure in Vietnam is so great that the government recognised that it was unable to do it all on its own. As a result, the government incentivised private companies to build. To pay for the projects, companies were given land.

Our investee did well for a time, but then something happened that we didn't see; there was a change in the law. In 2018, the government began to scrutinise these projects to assess both the process for handing over the land to companies like the one we invested in, as well as their value.

Many of these infrastructure companies did not tender the actual construction to credible companies; instead, they built roads, bridges and ports themselves, often with poor quality and at inflated costs. The government somehow wised up to this and realised these companies were inflating the construction costs to value the real estate exchanged. According to the law, the land should have gone to auction to maximise its value; that was not done. Subsequently, the government halted approval for the accounting of the construction of these projects. Meanwhile, the sponsor was selling his shares in the business, a form of money out.

Exceptions to the rule

The equitisation of an SOE is an example of money out; but in this case, it's the government sponsor taking the money and exiting, in whole or in part.

The CEO of a relatively recent investee of ours took money out, although she told us of her plan and it made sense. In general terms, the business she ran had two related but separate operations. At our direction, she split the company in two, and planned to use the money from the first one (in which we invested) to expand the second one (in which we did not invest).

Wait a minute, you are likely thinking, this not only violates the money-out rule but also the alignment of interests rule. We were not concerned because the CEO was transparent about her plan and she retains a significant majority stake in the first business, which is far larger than the second one will ever be. Because of that, we were confident that she would remain focused. That said, we paid a lower multiple for our stake and the risk was built into the return, so we will obviously keep a watchful eye for any signs of distraction. Equally, our growth commitment and associated drag-along penalty provided further assurance against the risk of defocus.

Another example of acceptable money out is a management buyout. This is the perfect private-equity deal, since you are aligned with someone who knows the most about the business and they have skin in the game. Unfortunately, there are very few opportunities for management buyouts in Vietnam – we have been involved in just one in nearly 20 years!

More than ten years ago, we backed the existing management of an international school to buy out the stake of the shareholder for a small price. The shareholder accepted the offer and sold the school to management with our capital because another potential buyer would not have been interested if the management team was not cooperative. There clearly was no alignment of interest between the shareholder and the management team, and we took full advantage of that dynamic to join with management and buy out the existing owner. Management borrowed some money from us and used the dividend from the school to repay us over a three-year period.

The takeaway

- With few exceptions, buyouts in particular, money out is a sign that something is wrong, or is about to go wrong, at your investee.

A side note about female CEOs in Vietnam

Many of Vietnam's top businesses are headed by women. Although I have not done a formal study of how the country compares to others, I would have to say that women lead more large companies in Vietnam than in most others. To those who have visited Vietnam, this may not come as a complete surprise. If you look at the small businesses in cities and towns around the country, you may have noticed that it is primarily women who run the stalls in the market, the shophouses, or restaurants. The Vietnamese entrepreneurial spirit has always been high, and women have been at the forefront of that.

Today, the prominence of female business executives is evident in some of Vietnam's largest and most successful companies.

Refrigeration Electrical Engineering Corporation, one of the first companies to list on the stock market in 2000, has been led by Madam Nguyen Thi Mai Thanh since its equitisation in 1993; it was also the first company to issue corporate bonds to foreign investors. Vinamilk has been led by women since it was founded in 1976, with female CEOs and chairwomen. DHG Pharmaceutical Joint-Stock Company, in which VOF was once a significant investor before selling our stake to Japan's Taisho Pharmaceutical, continues to be led by Madam Dang Thi Thu Ha.

Phu Nhuan Jewelry, Vietnam's leading jewellery retailer and a significant long-time VOF holding, continues to post strong growth under the leadership of Madam Cao Thi Ngoc Dung. And of course, the chairwoman of Vietjet, once known as the 'bikini airline', is Madam Nguyen Thanh Ha, who works alongside president and CEO Madam Nguyen Thi Phuong Thao, who also serves as vice chairman of HDBank and is one of Vietnam's wealthiest individuals. Several other banks and retailers have women at the helm. Meanwhile, some of the smaller companies in our portfolio were also founded and run by women, including Thu Cuc International Hospital in Hanoi, established and managed by Ms Nguyen Thu Cuc.

Thu Cuc International Hospital

These women have all been extremely effective in raising capital and growing their businesses. A common theme is that even when they bring in investors, they continue to hold significant stakes in the companies they run – their interests remain aligned with other shareholders. Most of all, they have remained focused even after their companies have grown and become successful. Although I am an equal opportunity investor, I will admit to having a higher level of confidence in companies run by women, at least until they give me reason otherwise.

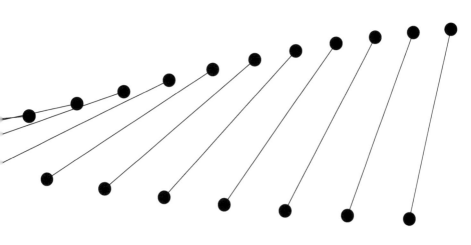

CHAPTER 5

TRUST BUT VERIFY: THE IMPORTANCE OF DUE DILIGENCE AND DOCUMENTATION

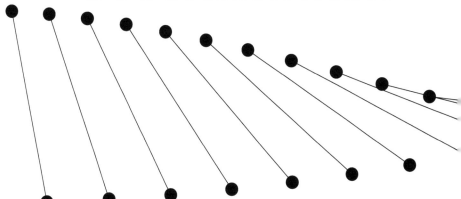

It was Lenin or Stalin who allegedly uttered the phrase, "trust, but verify". However, I remember it from when US President Ronald Reagan repeated it when discussing arms agreements with the Soviet President Mikhail Gorbachev.

A critical part of any major business deal is having the terms of discussion and negotiation committed to paper in the form of a document. Due diligence should be one of the most important parts of that process. You need to confirm what is being said and shown to you by a sponsor. Effectively, legal and financial due diligence is really an exercise in using third parties to validate or confirm your understanding of the business – and you don't expect to encounter any surprises.

In Vietnam even today, the Western investor might be surprised at how primitive due diligence and transaction documentation can be. Large corporate investigative firms, such as Kroll, FTI, or Control Risks, have only started operating in Vietnam in the past few years, and the kinds of services they have long offered in other parts of the world are just now starting to get traction here.

But until about a decade ago, the typical due diligence performed relative to a deal could perhaps be described as rudimentary. Trust is always at the foundation of business relationships here. Nevertheless, we have over time ramped up our due diligence capabilities.

Rule 11: Do not believe in the memories of entrepreneurs

In good times, people make all kinds of promises about their business, especially when they are trying to get you to invest. Entrepreneurs will typically make promises to you about three main areas:

1. **That everything related to the establishment of the company is in order** – business registration, licences, taxes, and so on. Everything is the way it is supposed to be.

2. **That they have proper corporate governance in place or are at least committed to putting it in place.** For example, they will have a defined level of authority for the board, CEO, directors and managers; and that the board will be involved in all material transactions and approving strategies, etc. Basically, they commit to having a series of checks and balances.

3. **That they can and will deliver on the growth commitments (revenue, profit, or EBITDA) you have set.**

Essentially, the entrepreneur will make a series of representations and warranties about the status of the business and commit to the targets and other changes the investor requires. They will say that they are a proper corporate citizen, paying the taxes owed, or that they follow basic ESG practices, or that they have a board that meets regularly to approve important corporate actions, such as taking out loans or raising equity.

Through due diligence, you will be able to confirm many of these statements, but not necessarily all of them. And there is a good chance that not all of them are quite true.

Perhaps the biggest and most common issue related to corporate establishment is taxes. Nobody in any country likes to pay taxes, but the Vietnamese system and its administration is notoriously complex and frustrating. That results in many, if not most, businesses maintaining two sets of books: one set of tax books and another of management books.

There are any number of ways a business can reduce its tax liability. But retaining earnings through questionable accounting becomes addictive and, left too long, will accumulate and become a significant liability. Few entrepreneurs will want to admit that they may have a potentially significant tax issue, especially to a potential investor! But such matters may not dissuade us from ultimately investing – if we know about them, we can factor that into a valuation and maybe even be able to help the company resolve the issue.

In terms of ESG-related issues, we sometimes find that investees have room for improvement, even if they are following the local laws and regulations. Local laws are still developing, particularly as they relate to environmental controls.

In one of our healthcare investments, our ESG consultant found that the amount of solid material being released into the river system was higher than what is standard in other parts of the world – although entirely acceptable by Vietnamese laws. As part of the investment documentation, we included a 'condition subsequent', or a commitment that the sponsor will implement a change after we invest, which required the company to upgrade its water filtration system and install a particular piece of equipment to sanitise the filtered material prior to its being properly disposed of. This is just one example of how our investment can lead to a positive change; we also have worked with investees to look at how much electricity they use and its source, as well as water usage.

Another area where we can seek change is corporate governance. With smaller family-run businesses, for example, we find that governance is not as robust as some founders make it out to be. The board may in fact be window dressing, comprised of other family members, and meet irregularly, if at all. The founder unilaterally decides what actions the company takes. That may work when it is purely a family business, but when outside investors get involved, that can no longer be the case.

In such circumstances, we will ask that governance be beefed up, and the founder will inevitably agree to our requests. They may even genuinely welcome such changes. Or they may be trying to pacify us, with no real intention of making changes. That's ok – we will put our changes in writing, and they will have to commit to them. And we will often bring in a third-party professional to sit on the board to improve corporate governance and ensure that these changes are made.

There are three types of independent board members we can bring on to the board of an investee:

1. **Retired operators**; with many years of experience in business, retired operators can be used to enhance management's ability to execute.

2. **Bankers** who have experience in business deals and finance; **academics**; or **accountants** who can help with audit matters.

3. **Senior statesman** who can serve as a face for the company, to investors, customers, or government officials.

Finally, there are the performance commitments that I described earlier. They are a critical part of our deals. Eager to have you invest, entrepreneurs may once again promise to meet them, perhaps not fully appreciating the work that will be necessary to achieve them. That's ok – we put it in writing, so we have the option of exercising the penalties if they are not met.

Properly document the representations and warranties, the agreements to improve governance, and performance targets and penalties, and you, the investor, will be well protected. Documentation provides an institutional memory, if you will, of what has been committed, even if the person you were dealing with is no longer there. These commitments to make changes are often referred to as 'conditions subsequent', and will be accompanied by default clauses in cases where they aren't carried out.

As an aside, you also want to be sure that your target has retained proper legal counsel and is receiving quality legal advice. You would think that if a founder was selling a stake in their company that they would. But that's not always been the case. We have come across instances where the sponsor relied on non-legal consultants or had lawyers who failed to communicate with all of the decision makers in a deal. To avoid a case of seller's remorse, the sponsor must have a knowledgeable lawyer who can fully understand and explain the consequences of a sale.

At this point, you are probably thinking to yourself that this is all very basic – of course you would want to document these kinds of issues in writing. In Vietnam, however, there is another very common dynamic among entrepreneurs, which is the matter of trust.

There is an old adage I learned, which is, "if you deal with a Chinese person in Chinatown, their word is binding". Basically, their promise is golden – they will follow through. Similarly, some Vietnamese entrepreneurs will ask why we have to go through all of these steps of documenting things and doing due diligence if you trust them as you say you do – of course they will fulfil their promises.

Indeed, there are a few entrepreneurs I know and have worked with who I know will do what they commit to doing. And if they can't, they will admit it and try to work with you to find a solution. But those individuals are rare, and the trust I have in them has been built over time, after they repeatedly demonstrated that they warranted that trust. Nevertheless, even when I do business with these people today, I still get commitments in writing!

Genesis of this rule

There is no single case that prompted this rule. It came about as the market started to mature and we saw the need to be more formal in our investments. There was an instance in which a transportation company whose corporate bond we purchased took money out to purchase real estate, and they did so without going through the board. That's because they didn't have a proper board, despite assuring us and other investors that they did. The real estate bubble burst, and the company was on the hook.

There are a couple of cases where our following this rule – demanding that promises be put in writing – prevented us from making what could have been some very big mistakes. About a decade ago, we were in discussions about investing in a language school. Education is one of our sectors of interest, as there is huge demand for private schools, especially in English centres. We drew up a term sheet documenting the performance commitments we expected for the valuation they wanted, just as we usually do. And then we waited. We later learned that they had taken the term sheet we drafted but removed the performance targets and found another foreign investor. And guess what – two years on and the school unsurprisingly was not performing, and the investor was left in a world of pain.

Another transportation company we were negotiating with did something similar about seven years ago – they took our term sheet, removed the commitments and the penalties, and found another foreign institution to buy into their dream. It didn't work out. These two instances demonstrate that sponsors have things that they don't want to put in writing. In both, our demand to fully document commitments resulted in investments not being made and, in the process, we avoided some negative outcomes.

The takeaway

- Entrepreneurs want you to buy into their dream and will promise things to you with the goal that you will do so. But investors have to be practical and documenting the entrepreneur's commitments will help prevent the dream from becoming a nightmare – at least for you.

Rule 12: Get official documents for all transactions

Vietnam is home to a complex bureaucratic system. Documents for seemingly very small tasks will require red stamps from one or more official or notaries. And of course, there is the ubiquitous 'red invoice', the only official receipt for products or services that prove that a company has paid the appropriate level of VAT. The red invoice is one of few official documents that have been digitised; for the most part, paper continues to rule the day.

Of course, when involved in a business transaction, you want all of the relevant documentation to be official. There are two critical levels of officiality that you want to look for:

1. **The company seal, or 'chop'**

2. **Notarisation**

The company chop, or official stamp, is one of the most important assets for operating a business. The stamps, which display the company's official name and registration number, certify that a company has authorised, for example, a payment, or published an official notice.

The stamp – which uses red ink by law – is placed over the signature of a company's legal representative, and documents featuring the combination of authorised signature and company chop are deemed legitimate and legally valid. The seals are registered with the police and must be kept secure at all times – they are difficult to replace if lost and a police report must be filed. An organisation may only have one seal; a duplicate of the original stamp must have a distinctive mark indicating that it is not the original. He who has the chop has the power!

Not long ago, there was a husband-and-wife team running a company in Vietnam. Their marriage fell apart, and the soon-to-be ex-wife ran off to Australia, company chop in hand. Her husband back in Vietnam was unable to transact company business, all because he did not have the corporate seal. One cannot simply walk over to the nearest stamp shop and ask to have a new one made!

The importance of the chop may fade over time. The most recent revision of the securities law, due to take effect in 2021, no longer requires businesses to register a sample of their stamp with the Business Registration Authority. Meanwhile, a survey conducted by the Vietnam Chamber of Commerce and Industry found that half of companies agreed that company seals should be abolished. And just as Japan is starting drastic reforms around the use of its version of the chop, called the *hanko*, I would expect Vietnam to eventually implement some form of digital chop in the years ahead.

Other documents must be certified or notarised – simple photocopies without the appropriate red stamps of notaries and government offices are far less valuable and have a much lower legal standing in a dispute. The point of all these official stamps and seals is to triangulate information – it is not simply one document that is proper, it is the whole set that tells the whole story behind the individual, company, or transaction.

It's not just companies that have issues with official documentation, but also SOEs. One large state-owned bank, Agribank, owns a large amount of land – mainly land on which its branches are, or were, located. At some point, the government gave Agribank an ultimatum: use the land or return it. The question then came to valuing the land, so that Agribank could sell it to a third party or otherwise have a baseline for negotiating price with the relevant government agency.

However, there was one big problem. Agribank did not possess official documentation for many of its properties, preventing it from selling or transferring it back to the government! Part of this may relate to a legacy war issue – many official records in the south were lost or destroyed in 1975. Nevertheless, this issue around the land has held up Agribank's equitisation as it is difficult to devise a proper valuation of the bank.

The takeaways

- The importance of the chop stems from a reliance on bureaucracy, a still-developing legal and commercial system, along with modern technology that makes it easier to forge signatures and documents. The chop – and any embossment – helps prevent fraud.

- Always insist on official documentation with the requisite red stamps – if a company cannot produce them, consider walking away.

Rule 13: Perform health and background checks on key executives

When you are investing in a private business, it is likely that the founder is the CEO and the business is their baby. It has reached a level of success that she or he is proud of, and as the investor, you are banking on the fact that she or he will continue to be involved – you're trusting in them and their experience (Rule 3). Accordingly, as the investor, you want to be sure of who you're dealing with and that they will be around to grow the business through the period of your investment.

Although it is commonplace in the West for CEOs of big corporations to have board-mandated health checks, it is still relatively rare in Vietnam. Years ago, we were presented with an opportunity to invest in a wire company called Ngo Han. We conducted our due diligence and were in the process of finalising the investment when the CEO died from cancer, and there was no obvious successor. We were silently upset by the fact that the CEO never shared with us that he had this illness well in advance of our engagement, and at that time, we never would have thought to ask that he have a health check.

But that is now a regular requirement, as well as a disclosure about insurance policies. We did not end up investing in the company because the key person to lead it was no longer there. We also now place greater importance on the 'key man' issue and health risks.

Background checks are also a relatively recent phenomenon in Vietnam. Of course, we have always looked into whether a prospective investee had criminal convictions or other legal troubles, but today it goes well beyond that. We want to know about things that suggest that there could be trouble in the future, even if nothing has happened in the past.

We want to know, for example, if the founder's or CEO's lifestyle is consistent with what we would expect it to be. If we find that a CEO of an SOE drives a Maybach, lives in a villa, and sends his children to private schools, we are going to be alarmed; in theory, he should not be able to afford such luxuries on a state salary. But there may be legitimate sources of wealth that enable him to do so, such as family money. In any case, such findings warrant further investigation prior to investing.

When considering investing in a private company, issues like those are less important because state assets are not involved. But again, we would want to make sure that the lifestyle is commensurate with the wealth. If it does not align, it could be a sign of gambling, misappropriating corporate funds, or transferring corporate assets to personal use. Again, the alignment of interest issue is at the fore.

We also want to know something about past civil disputes – what were they about and how were they resolved? A potential investee's personal relationships are also telling, especially in a family business. Do they have a stable family life? Who is their extended family and how do they get on with them? What is their background? Is there potential political exposure?

This is a lesson we learned the hard way. There was one company in which we invested that was run by a respected maternal figure. She built the company up and was looking to sell us a stake. Her entire family was involved in the business – her siblings, her children – and given that the company was performing well, we did not give this much thought. It appeared to be an example of a very successful family business.

However, after investing, we discovered that all was not as happy as it might have appeared. While the founder was very generous with her siblings – she always provided for their homes and education like a mother, for example – some of the extended family were resentful of her. They always had to go to her, hat in hand, to ask for her support, and the frustration grew over time. Family members did not have stakes in the business but were instead promised half the proceeds if and when the founder sold her entire stake to a third party.

It turned out that one of the founder's brothers had been negotiating a control deal with a large international company, and the brother was not at all pleased with the founder's deal with us. The relative's deal would have allowed him and the other members of the extended family to receive significant amounts in the near term, while our deal came with our usual performance commitments and expectations over time. The brother and some of his siblings wanted to get out of the business. A number of other issues surfaced, and we ultimately withdrew our investment, receiving our cash back with interest. Incidentally, because of the issues that surfaced, the international company the brother had been negotiating with was no longer interested in buying the company either.

Extended family issues like the example above are relatively rare. But we certainly dig deeper into family matters as a result. One of the key relationships we want to know something about is the status of a sponsor's marriage.

The takeaway

- Background and health checks are still not that prevalent in business deals in Vietnam, although that is slowly changing. They are especially important in smaller companies, where the lines of succession are not so clear and the depth of talent in the company is shallow. Taking the added step of looking into a person's legal, business, and medical history may allow you to avoid some messy situations later.

Rule 14: Husbands and wives do get divorced – consider it carefully when investing in a family business

Acceptance of divorce is rising in Vietnam, and today the divorce rate reported by the HCMC courts stands at about 30%.[5] Not quite the 50% of places like the US, but it is rising. As such, divorce is an important factor to consider when investing in a family business.

As mentioned in the previous rule, we will typically conduct a background check to ascertain the status of a marriage.

---

5 "Marry in haste, repent at leisure – Vietnam's changing marital dynamics", *Xinhua*, 5 December 2018.

Whether both husband and wife are involved in the operation of the business is one issue; another is ownership.

Most private businesses in Vietnam are family businesses, and many of those we come across have a husband-and-wife team running the show. More often than not, the wife is the one who handles the money (and is usually quite good at it), while the husband tends to focus on strategy and operations.

In 2018, a husband-and-wife team who owned a successful local restaurant business approached us about a potential investment in their company, which operates several casual-dining venues. They were looking to expand.

Through our discussions, we quickly learned that their relationship was intense, and that they were at each other's throats about every issue related to running the business. For example, the husband wanted to hire a professional who had no experience in the restaurant sector to handle marketing, while the wife insisted on someone with restaurant experience. The wife played a more active role in the business – she ran the day-to-day operations while the husband handled strategy. Staff were confused about the leadership too – the husband would order something to be done and the wife would contradict him. It was an untenable situation.

As it was clear they were headed for divorce, we suggested to the wife that she buy out her soon-to-be ex-husband, which she ultimately did. Problem solved? No. Some restaurants closed, and EBITDA plummeted, and she was now looking for investors. As good as she was at managing the books, she was not able to handle the operations side of the business. We decided not to invest.

Case study: Trung Nguyen Coffee – A marriage goes sour

Earlier in this book, I mentioned a company called Trung Nguyen Coffee as one of the few examples of a Vietnamese company that successfully transformed into an exporter. Founded in 2006, Trung Nguyen Corporation JSC grew to become the top coffee company in Vietnam.

Trung Nguyen G7 coffee on sale in store

Credit: Dragfyre (obtained via Wikimedia Commons)

In 2017, Trung Nguyen Coffee earned revenue of over $170m and profit after tax of $29m.[6] It is involved in coffee production, processing, and distribution, and exports to more than 60 markets around the world. It operates various subsidiaries,

---

6 "Vietnam's Coffee King loses control in company to wife", *VN Express*, 17 July 2016.

including the Trung Nguyen Instant Coffee Company JSC, as well as having a chain of branded cafes throughout the country, and franchises in several countries. By all accounts, Trung Nguyen was a success story – that rare Vietnamese company that truly went global.

But we have to go back eight years before the company was founded, to 1998. That year, Dang Le Nguyen Vu married Le Hoang Diep Thao. The couple co-founded Trung Nguyen Coffee, and would later be anointed the Coffee King and Coffee Queen respectively by the local press. The King owned 20% of the company, the Queen 10%, with the remaining 70% held by Trung Nguyen Investment Corporation, which was owned by the couple as well as other investors.

When the company was founded, the King served as chairman and CEO, while the Queen was appointed deputy general director. By most accounts, she was the more active half of the couple in the company's operations. For many years, the business empire expanded nicely. But all was not well – something caused the Queen to file for divorce from the King in 2015.

Two years earlier, in 2013, the King retreated to the mountains in Vietnam to meditate, a sojourn that would last for nearly five years. While the King was meditating, the Queen ran the company, and quite successfully at that: the company's charter capital increased from $6.5m to nearly $109m as well as recording impressive revenue and profit growth.

After the divorce filing, the King ousted the Queen from the company. The divorce precipitated a complex legal crisis for the company, with a rollercoaster of developments. The King removed the Queen from her role as chairman and general manager of the instant coffee subsidiary, which the Queen said was not authorised; a provincial court sided with her. In 2018, she accused senior executives at the parent company of forging signatures on corporate documents. The twists and turns were covered extensively in the media.

In June 2018, the King "came down from the mountains" and made a "surprise" appearance at a company event. He stated that the Trung Nguyen team needed to "revolutionize" themselves and "aim to become the number one coffee brand in the world, establishing its presence everywhere". He said the five years meditating had given him "answers to all the questions in this world".[7] Perhaps unsurprisingly, the Queen petitioned the divorce court to have the King's mental health assessed – a request that was rejected.

The court issued its final ruling in the divorce in December 2019, giving the King 60% of the shared assets (valued at an estimated $245m) and control of the group; the Queen had petitioned for 51% ownership in her favour. Properties were to be split equally. Recognising that dividing the company's shares would create difficulties in the company's ongoing operation, the court ordered that the King would buy out the Queen's 40% in cash, or about $51m, as well as pay her several million dollars in cash and gold. The King was also ordered to pay the soon-to-be former Queen $431,000 a year to support her in raising their four children.[8]

---

7 "Vietnam's Coffee King comes down from the mountain", *VN Express*, 19 June 2018.

8 "Coffee King to manage Trung Nguyen empire after divorce, court says", *VN Express*, 27 March 2019.

Meanwhile, the company suffered. In 2018, profit fell 50%, to $15m, a clear indicator that the divorce drama caused the company's leadership to lose focus on the business. The former Queen has gone on to start her own coffee brand, King Coffee – an interesting name.

This is an extreme example, to be sure. The media attention this soap opera of a divorce received usually only happens with celebrities. But the Trung Nguyen drama clearly and publicly illustrates the risks entailed with investing in a business owned and operated by a married couple.

We've been lucky to not have experienced a divorce-related issue in our own investments. But if we had concerns about the stability of an investee's marriage, we might negotiate a provision in the deal documentation that would allow for either us or an independent trustee to be appointed to handle stock ownership prior to a ruling of a divorce court should the marriage come to an end.

The takeaway

- Investing in a company owned and/or operated by a married couple carries significant added risk and a potential complication: divorce. It is imperative that we have an understanding of the couple's dynamics prior to getting involved. As mentioned earlier, successful male CEOs commonly have one or more mistresses, and so they do veer off-course. As such, divorces are not uncommon.

Rule 15: When in doubt, put it in the assumption section of the letter of intent or term sheet

When evaluating a potential investment, we do our best to ascertain the facts about a company using publicly available information (which may be limited or non-existent in the case of a private company) as well as our own independent research and analysis. We of course ask the sponsor for information, but sometimes the required information is not forthcoming, or as specific as we would like. There is a degree of information asymmetry we deal with and try to level out as best as possible.

We use the assumption section of the letter of intent or term sheet to learn as much as possible about the way a business operates. For example, when investing in a family business, the roles of individual family members may not be clear, nor is ownership of the shares. These are crucial pieces of information. Where we don't have a clear picture, we will make educated guesses in the form of statements in the assumption section. Those guesses are usually wrong, but the sponsor will have to correct them.

This is a common practice of journalism in Vietnam. Sometimes a reporter will call you for comment about something, you aren't interested in taking their call, so the reporter will publish an article with his assumptions – which are usually incorrect, inaccurate, or otherwise wrong – and you will then be compelled to call him back and correct his reporting!

Say there is a family business you are interested in investing in. The father is the chairman and the son is the CEO. We would want to know if the son owns shares, or does the father hold them all? What happens if the father dies – could he perhaps leave all his shares to his daughters? What would happen to the CEO son in such a scenario? The possibilities are almost endless, and many of them are not pretty.

Some of the other standard statements we like to put in this section include:

- Stating that the CEO is in good health and has had a medical check-up in the past 12 months (easier than asking them to have a health check right off the bat).

- That none of the management team has a criminal record and that they are not being investigated for any criminal activity.

- That there have been no discussions of divorce or other family conflicts that could potentially disrupt the business.

- The financial statements have been prepared under VAS (Vietnam accounting standards) or IFRS (international financial reporting standards).

- Use of funding.

The fact that we list these sorts of questions does not mean that we aren't doing our best to independent verify such matters – we do. But again, with a private family-run business, public information is likely limited. Additionally, we may discover that the potential investee was not truthful in answering the questions, in which case we would have to start questioning whether they can be trusted.

The takeaway

- If you are unable to obtain the level of information you need to be comfortable with proceeding with an investment, put your best guesses in the assumption section – the sponsor should review that section and correct any inaccurate statements.

Rule 16: Any promise can be broken if it is not written down in a signed document

This rule is self-evident. But one consideration in Vietnam is to have all documentation prepared in English *and* Vietnamese, with *both* versions signed.

Most of my team speak Vietnamese, and we mostly deal with our target companies in Vietnamese. Accordingly, documents are prepared in that language. Of course, it is easier for some of my non-Vietnamese speaking colleagues to have documents translated into English. But that's not the point of this rule.

In our deal documentation, we typically stipulate that disputes are to be arbitrated in Singapore or Hong Kong, where the legal system is more independent, transparent, and experienced in complex corporate legal matters. As such, our international lawyers would require documents in English.

There are a number of cases where we do rely on the Vietnam International Arbitration Center. In its early years, it was considered relatively easy to influence the three-person panel that would decide the outcome of a dispute. But this has changed over time, and the quality of the dispute-resolution forum has improved significantly. This largely came about as more foreign lawyers got involved – people who have good reputations and are well paid are less likely to risk their licences to practice. That being the case, we do still tend to use Singapore or Hong Kong, given the breadth and depth of their expertise.

Documents are prepared in both languages and signed at the same time so that all parties can ensure that there are no mistranslations or misunderstandings.

This has been our practice for as long as I can recall, so I do not remember the genesis of this rule. However, there was a dispute with a sponsor not so long ago, who claimed that the English documentation varied from the Vietnamese documentation. That was not the case, and the claim further underscored the difficulty of working with this party. We successfully withdrew from the investment and our principal was returned in full.

The takeaway

- It is easier to prepare for possible disputes before they might arise.

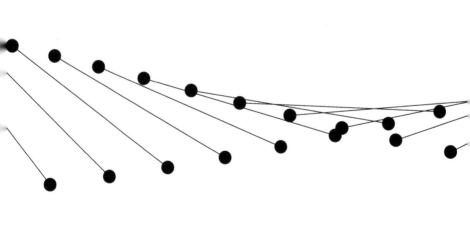

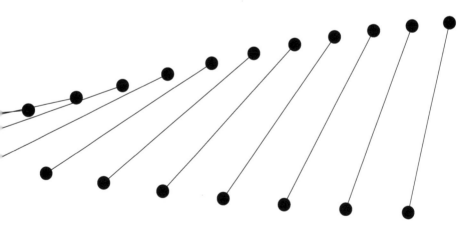

CHAPTER 6

GETTING OUT: EXIT CONSIDERATIONS

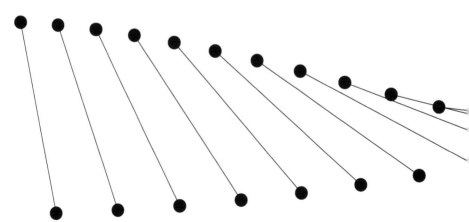

As investors, we are always planning a way out of our investments. After all, we don't make money until we exit an investment. Ideally, our exit comes three to five years after our investee has achieved or surpassed the agreed upon growth targets, and the company lists on the stock exchange or is sold to a strategic buyer. Or notes have matured, and we make a nice return for our shareholders. All involved have benefitted and made good money in the process.

Over a four year period, from 2010 to 2013, we averaged one major trade sale per quarter. In 2014, we took some companies public, as the stock market became a more viable way to exit. These days, trade sales are once again the most common exit and we have executed several successful deals over the past few years.

Sometimes, however, our exit comes under less-than-ideal circumstances. Usually that relates to the investee being unable to meet the performance commitments they made, and we are exercising one of the four penalties. In these situations, our first preference is to get the sponsor back to the table and find a mutually beneficial way forward. Failing that, we will divest and move on.

Rule 17: Always have an exit clause, even if you have to pay a penalty

We always aim to have an orderly exit from an investment in a business. If a company is listed on the stock exchange, the exit is easy: we sell the shares and are done with it. But private equity is capital invested in an illiquid instrument. Getting out isn't so easy. Just like when flying on an airplane, you always need to know where the exit is and where the parachutes are stored.

We typically view investments with a three- to five-year investment horizon. That's because in a frontier market like Vietnam, it is difficult to know what is going to happen three years in the future, so we like to have an off-ramp available to us if needed. If a company is performing well, we may hold on to that investment longer, maybe for five, seven, or even ten years, if we believe it is beneficial to our investors to do so.

In the best-case scenarios, our investees do well and we are able to get them to list on the stock exchange or sell to a strategic buyer. These are win-win situations.

In an IPO, you have to prepare the company for listing. It helps if they have strong retail-brand recognition. If you're going to list a company, you should be focusing on mobilising money from retail investors (i.e., the general public). Our long-time investee, PNJ, the country's largest jeweller, was easy to take public – everyone in Vietnam knew of the company. Airlines are also easy because of their familiarity.

On the other side of the coin are industrial companies and companies in the business-to-business sector, whose brands are not widely known by the general public. That doesn't mean they shouldn't go public; it's just a bigger challenge.

Another long-time holding of ours is steelmaker Hoa Phat Group. The average consumer doesn't buy steel and has never heard of the company. But they wanted to go public, even though they could have sold to another steelmaker. They listed in 2007 and have done very well (especially in 2020), although their stock trades at a lower single-digit multiple. Vinamilk, which delivers profit after tax of around $500m, trades with a P/E in the low 20s.

Hoa Phat steel mill

Source: Hoa Phat Group

Stock markets, particularly in frontier countries, are volatile and unpredictable. Those lower-profile companies are usually more suitable for a sale to a strategic buyer, for which there has been no dearth in Vietnam. A number of large international companies, such as CJ, Taisho and Diageo, have done deals in Vietnam, eager to establish a presence in this growing market.

In preparing for a strategic sale, we would help the company prepare by strengthening their capabilities in the three core areas buyers look for in potential acquisitions. As I mentioned earlier, these are: an established brand; established distribution channels; and manufacturing capability and scalability.

One of our earliest investments was in a vodka company called Halico. Their Hanoi Vodka brand was well known, if not particularly well regarded. But it was priced right. At the time of investment, we did not believe that Halico would make an ideal listed company being that it focused only on vodka. But we did see it as a good target for a strategic buyer. As such, we embarked on a plan to develop all three core areas – brand, distribution channels, and manufacturing scalability. We also focused on lowering the product cost by changing the bottles from glass to PET (a common plastic bottle material). This helped drive sales and distribution as cost savings were spent on marketing.

In 2011, we sold the company to a strategic buyer, Diageo. It was clear that Halico's brands were less important to the international drinks giant, and that the established distribution networks and manufacturing capabilities were the draw. Diageo subsequently increased its stake to 45%.

In cases where something goes awry and the sponsor is unable to perform as promised, we have four penalties (cash back, share top-up, put option, or drag along) to fall back on. It is always important to have options – if the sponsor can't do option A or B, there is always C. As an example, say you want to exercise the put option, whereby the sponsor is obligated to buy back your stake at cost plus interest. If he says he can't buy, that obligation goes away, and you move to the next option.

The takeaways

- Have a plan on day one of your investment as to how you are going to eventually exit it, be it the best-case scenario or the worst – have a path out. Having options mitigates the potential downsides.

- Focus on creating value where it will be most beneficial to increase the worth of the business and enhance the exit probability.

Rule 18: Control your money to leverage your position

In 2008, we invested in a large local bank, acquiring a 5% stake via a private placement. It was one of the largest banks in Vietnam and generally well regarded, such that a Japanese investor had earlier purchased a 15% stake. However, two things went very wrong.

As we finalised the terms of our investment, we put our money into an escrow account – I will get back to that in a moment. As we continued to negotiate, we learned more and more about how the bank was operating, and we grew concerned about some of what we were learning.

When we initiated the investment, we did not conduct a thorough due diligence. However, the Japanese investor had prior to its investment shortly before ours, and we relied on the fact that they had invested and went along with their valuation. Big mistake.

One of the terms the bank insisted on was something we were not prepared to take on, and we questioned whether the Japanese investor would have agreed to it. As it turned out, they were not concerned. As strategic investors with a long-term view, they had other rights. On top of that, Japanese investors are not usually eager to change things that have already been agreed on as that can cause a loss of face, something that is culturally frowned upon.

Now, as these discoveries and negotiations were under way, the share price of most banks started to tumble, eventually falling around an average of 20%. Back in 2004 and 2005, the shares of banks were very popular among investors. In my earlier role at Prudential, we invested $50m in five banks, including the one we wanted to invest in now. Over the next two, three, four years, the price of bank shares went up between 5–10 times, depending on the bank. Coincidentally, when we were negotiating with this bank in 2007, my former employer, Prudential, started to liquidate its bank portfolio, driving share price down.

Again, as a strategic investor, the Japanese company was not concerned. But for us, the share price fall caused havoc. We wanted our money back to renegotiate the terms, but the bank ignored us. Ultimately, we were able to reach an agreement and things eventually worked out – we made money on our investment, though we could have made a lot more.

Now back to that money in escrow. Can you guess at which bank the escrow account was held?

That's right, the sponsor. This was at their insistence. They earned interest on our capital as it sat in escrow for several months. Since then, we have always insisted that escrow accounts be held at a bank that has no relationship to the target. That can be difficult in Vietnam, as the community is quite small and there are a range of complicated relationships – some in the open, some not so visible. For example, it is well known that conglomerate Masan Group has a significant stake in Techcombank; we obviously would not set up an escrow account there if we were trying to do a deal with Masan (not that I am suggesting that Techcombank has done or would do anything improper).

These days, we typically insist on escrow accounts being held at one of the large state-owned commercial banks, like Vietcombank, or one of the international bank branches, such as Standard Chartered or Citibank.

In Vietnam, escrow is not as clear-cut as it is in other countries where, generally speaking, if the conditions of a transaction are met in a certain time frame, say 90 days, the buyer's money is transferred to the seller automatically. Conversely, if the seller fails to meet its obligations, the money is returned to the buyer. Here, no matter the outcome, all three parties – the buyer, the seller, and the bank – have to sign off on the release of funds. As you may have surmised, this creates a potentially difficult situation.

The law blames the bank if the other parties fail to reach agreement on releasing funds. As such, the international banks will conduct a level of due diligence around the establishment of escrow accounts – they want to know who they are dealing with and whether they can be trusted.

The takeaway

- Having some control over your money provides critical leverage when negotiating (or renegotiating) terms – do not cede control until you are comfortable with the deal. And if you use escrows, insist on an independent, preferably international, bank.

Rule 19: Think three times when exercising a convertible loan

Sometimes we will invest in a company via a convertible loan or bond, under which we will have the option to convert the loan or bond into equity in the business. If the company is performing well, converting a loan or bond into equity sounds like a good deal, right? It may be, but you have to think *three* times before proceeding. In other words, think very carefully about the ramifications of converting. Once you convert, you've lost optionality, and optionality is valuable – you want that to last as long as possible.

Convertible loans or bonds can offer the potential of 'equity upside' along with the 'downside protections' we want. For example, if the business is not performing as well as expected, you know you have your exit – when the loan or bond matures and you are paid back principal plus the negotiated interest rate. That essentially is the put option, one of our four standard downside protections.

If the business is performing well, it may make sense to continue your investment and convert to equity. But before doing so you should think carefully – you are narrowing your options for exiting.

The terms of these convertible products are usually 2–3 years, and we usually have the option to convert any time before they mature. But while you may potentially see more upside as a shareholder, the dynamics have changed.

For example, your rights as a shareholder are below those of a debt holder, and you may have lost collateral. You have most likely lost any leverage you may have had to negotiate with or provide input to the company on how it should be managed, and you will have likely lost visibility into how the company is governed or whether it will undertake a liquidity event like an IPO. Conversion to a minority equity stake does not allow you to inherit minority rights or protections. You could try to obtain minority rights when converting, but there really is no good reason for the sponsor to accede to that request – you have become just another minority shareholder.

Apart from wanting to retain a stake in a company that is doing well, there are some other scenarios where it may make sense to convert. We just have to think one, two, three times about the potential upsides. Examples include:

- Say you hold a convertible bond in a company, and for whatever reason, you want to exit now. You know that there is a potential strategic buyer in the market, so you convert to equity and find someone to take your share.

- Bonds are collateralised with fixed assets, like land or buildings, or shares in the company (though that is not very meaningful in a private company). The sponsor may ask you to release collateral to raise capital. Do you? Of course not, it secures the bond. However, if you convert to equity, the need for collateral goes away. In this case, you have some bargaining power – the sponsor needs the collateral back – and you have the opportunity to negotiate minority rights and protections. It may make sense, but think it through!

The cases that prompted the rule

Several years ago, we made a convertible loan to a company that developed several successful mixed-use properties in HCMC. The company was doing well, having constructed several large complexes in the city. The decision was made to convert, which gave us a stake of about 6% equity in the privately held company.

Since converting, we asked for information and pushed management to make changes. For example, we would like to see them do an IPO. But as much as we kicked and screamed, our demands fell on deaf ears. They ignored us and continued to operate the company as they liked.

Because the company is private, it is extraordinarily difficult to sell our stake to someone else. Our options are very limited. Fortunately, the company continues to perform well – but how and when we eventually get out remains a question mark. Someone clearly did not think three times before converting!

Other cases

More recently, we converted a loan into equity which resulted in our having a controlling stake. It was a difficult turnaround, involving bringing in new management and restructuring the company. Although we were eventually able to make a successful exit via a sale to a strategic buyer, the experience took far more time, money, and effort than we ever would have expected. We should have thought two or three more times about whether converting was the right move.

There are many mundane cases of conversion too. In one investee, we have an outstanding bond that we are considering converting because of the potential for a transaction. In another company, we converted to equity simply because they went public and could not have outstanding bonds.

In Vietnam, there is an added complication as it relates to convertible bonds. When they are sold to a foreign investor, the converted equity stake that would be obtained affects the company's FOL. This can cause issues in companies that are near or at their limits.

The takeaway

- Options are valuable. When considering converting a loan or a bond to equity, think it through very, very carefully – there may be good potential upside, but once you exercise that right, your options for exiting may be extremely limited.

Rule 20: Don't take control; use the drag-along right

As mentioned in Rule 2, we have a number of downside protections at our disposal to use if an investee fails to meet their performance commitments. One of those is the drag-along right. This provision allows us to take some of the sponsor's equity stake and add it to our stake to sell a minimum of 51% to a buyer looking for a controlling stake. Of the four penalties, this is one of the most difficult to use. But in the final analysis, it can result in a positive outcome for all involved.

Consider the other penalties first: it is unlikely that the sponsor has the cash to return our investment to us if we exercised a rebate or put-option clause. If we were to take a share top-up, we could increase our stake to 51% or more, and we would technically have control of the company. However, we really have no interest in managing the company – that's not our specialty. It's difficult and time consuming, and on top of that, we would become responsible for the company's representations, warrants and contingent liabilities.

In previous chapters, I have mentioned some of the challenges surrounding CEO recruitment. A further reason why it is difficult to find new CEOs in the local market, especially at companies in some degree of distress, is that the CEO is the legal representative of a company, and economic crimes in Vietnam can lead to prosecution. Taking control is something we want to avoid at most costs.

At the end of the day, we are a financial investor. We rely on the sponsor and their ability to operate the business they built and meet the performance goals that have been set. If the sponsor and their team were unable to meet the performance goals, we are unlikely to do so either.

The drag along is useful for initiating a sale of the business. We prefer to work with existing management teams to get a business to a place where it is marketable and attractive to a strategic buyer. A 51% stake tends to be the minimum to attract such buyers, and they are willing to pay an ever greater premium for an even larger one, such as a 66% supermajority stake that would enable them to make management and structural changes without putting them to a shareholder vote.

Immediately after a sale is closed, there are at least two happy parties: the buyer, who has acquired a business that will help it grow in the market, and the investor, who was able to effectuate an exit amid challenging circumstances and deliver a return to their own investors. The sponsor – despite likely having received a premium for the shares they owned – may not initially see things the same way. After all, this was their baby, so to speak, the company that in all likelihood they spent a good part of their lives building; they may blame you, the investor, for taking it away from them. But once the dust settles and they look at the situation rationally, they too tend to look at the outcome as a positive.

Although I have provided examples and anecdotes throughout the book, there are two cases in particular that demonstrate how many of the rules come into play.

Case study: Huy Vietnam Group

Source: Huyvietnam.com

The years 2014 and 2015 were heady times for the Huy Vietnam Group (HVG). The then seven-year-old restaurant chain, founded by Vietnamese-American Huy Nhat, announced that it had raised $30m in Series B and Series C[9] equity financing to help expand the number of stores and brands it operated.

Over the course of three fundraising rounds, from the company's start to April 2015, HVG reportedly raised a total of $65m[10] from a variety of international private-equity firms and family offices, including AIF Capital, Fortress Capital, Welkin, and Templeton Asset Management (then led by emerging-markets investment pioneer Mark Mobius).

Notice anything? I will get back to that.

These experienced American, Singaporean, Hong Kong, and Chinese investment firms were no doubt swayed by Vietnam's growth story, as well as HVG's polished presentation and story. It operated dozens of restaurants, mainly under the brands 'Mon Hue', which served foods from the central region of Vietnam, and 'Pho Ong Hung', which served pho. According to press releases, the company, which was incorporated in Hong Kong, claimed to be "one of the first international, professionally managed restaurant chains operated in Vietnam serving traditional Vietnamese food prepared from formulated family recipes".[11]

---

9 Series A, B, and C rounds of fundraising relate to various stages of capital raising to finance a business. Series A funding will typically come after a start-up has some sort of track record; Series B and C will typically occur at businesses that have achieved some level of success but require capital to grow further and take things to the 'next level'.

10 "Vietnamese restaurant chains attract foreign investors", *Thanh Nien News*, 27 June 2016.

11 "Huy Vietnam Secures Series C Equity Financing of US$15.0 million for Restaurant Chain Expansion in Vietnam", *PRNewswire*, 13 April 2015.

Dennis Nguyen, vice chairman of HVG and chairman of New Asia Partners, a Minneapolis- or Hong Kong-based PE firm depending on the reporting, and HVG's first institutional investor,[12] noted in the Series B press release that a representative of AIF Capital would join the board to "add value through corporate governance", while Fortress Capital would help in "capital markets intelligence and investor relations".[13] By the end of 2015, it was reported that HVG planned an initial public offering in Hong Kong to raise an additional $100m, a rumour the company denied.[14]

For the next two years, it seemed as if business was going well for HVG. The company did indeed expand from 40 restaurants in late 2014 to 140 by mid-2017. The company was featured in a *Nikkei* (Japanese news service) article about the growth of Vietnamese restaurant chains giving "visitors a taste of authenticity".[15]

For another two years, there was little news about the company. All around HCMC, one could see new Mon Hue and Pho Ong Hung restaurants opening, or old locations being renovated. Things were seemingly moving forward, if more quietly than in previous years.

Over time, it seems that Mr Huy expanded his interests and became director of another company called the Horizon Property Group Company, which was "pitching a resort

---

12 "Foreign investors sue Huy Vietnam founder for alleged $25m fraud", *DealStreetAsia*, 25 May 2020.

13 "Huy Vietnam Closes US$15.0 million Series B Financing for Restaurant Chain Expansion in Vietnam", *PRNewswire*, 28 September 2014.

14 "Dining chains operator Huy Vietnam rejects overseas IPO report", *Thanh Nien*, 10 December 2015.

15 "Vietnam chain eateries give visitors a taste of authenticity", *Nikkei*, 24 May 2017.

development project, Horizon Langco, in central Vietnam".[16] Once again, Mr Huy was pitching to foreign investors for investment in his latest project.

By the second half of 2019, it suddenly appeared that things were amiss at HVG. In October of that year, Mon Hue restaurants suddenly started closing. The one across the street from our office, located in the heart of HCMC, closed one day with a sign suggesting the closure was temporary. Literally, one day it was operating normally and the next it was closed. This scene played out across the city and country.

Concerned about what they were witnessing, a number of the company's vendors picketed outside the HGV corporate headquarters in HCMC, demanding to be paid debts by Mon Hue they claimed have been owed for months. The HVG website suddenly went dark, and the local news reported that no employees were seen in the corporate offices. The media attention prompted the local tax authorities to review their records – they found that the firm owed billions of VND in VAT.

Just a few days after posting the 'temporary closure' sign on the location across from our office, construction workers were inside tearing out the fixtures, the 'Mon Hue' sign covered with 'for rent' flyers.

While the closures appeared sudden, there were a few signs that something irregular was occurring at the company. In early October 2019 – a couple of weeks before the closures – the company changed its legal representative from Mr Huy to someone called Nguyen Quynh Anh. HVG's charter capital

---

16 "Huy Vietnam, Coteccons highlight governance risks for overseas investors", *DealStreetAsia*, 17 August 2020.

was cut in half to $25.9m, while the subsidiary operating Mon Hue saw its charter capital increase more than 30 times to $28.3m.

According to reporting by *VnExpress*, a local newspaper, between 2016 and 2019, Mon Hue lost nearly $5m as it expanded. In 2016, it made a $12,950 profit, but for each of the subsequent two years, lost $2.2m. Its reported gross profit margin in both 2017 and 2018 was up to 68%, although selling expenses accounted for 80–90% of revenue.[17]

At the end of October 2019, six of the PE firms that had invested in HVG filed a lawsuit against Mr Huy, claiming he closed the restaurants without seeking their approval, and that he allegedly breached fiduciary duties, executed unusual transactions, and committed fraud. They also claimed they had obtained court orders freezing Mr Huy's assets overseas.

In early and mid-2020, another group of firms – those who invested in the resort project that never materialised – also filed suit alleging fraud and seeking that Mr Huy be barred from leaving Vietnam as well as prosecuted. In their lawsuit, they noted that Mr Huy had "dispersed most of the appropriated assets by transferring properties to his family members, asked his accountant … to withdraw cash from the accounts of Horizon Vietnam and Mon Hue and then deposit it [in] Huy Nhat's personal accounts."[18] To my knowledge, the legal actions are still pending, and Mr Huy has not been arrested or prosecuted. In fact, his whereabouts seem to be a mystery.

---

17 "Restaurant chain Mon Hue keeps losing millions of dollars", *VnExpress*, 24 October 2019.

18 "Four foreign investors ask for arrest of Huy Nhat over fraud violations", *Hanoi Times*, 11 July 2020.

At the start of this case study, I asked if anything seemed peculiar. What should raise a warning is the fact that all of the investors are from overseas – there is not a single local firm that invested in these rounds of fundraising! VinaCapital was casually approached about investing in HVG years ago, and I suspect other firms were too. We took a pass for several reasons, but one of the most important was the fact that their restaurants were usually empty – the food was mediocre at best, and relatively expensive compared to the same dishes served on the street.

HVG provides a good example of how some of the rules can prevent investment mistakes. Clearly interests were not aligned, although I can't say whether we would have found reason to trust Mr Huy, nor can I say whether background checks might have found anything that might have tipped us off about what was to come. There was money going out for real estate, if not for outright fraudulent purposes.

Most importantly, HVG speaks of the need to play an active role in PE investments in Vietnam, to act as a check-and-balance analyst and monitor what is happening in real time, not after the fact. From public reports, this would appear to be a clear case of fraud, and I certainly sympathise with the investors and wish them luck in their legal cases. However, I cannot help but think that they should have known things were going awry sooner than they did.

Case study: DairyCo

It was a particularly hot and humid day in May 2013, and I remember vividly walking from our office to the Park Hyatt Saigon to take a first meeting with the chairman of DairyCo, Mr Manh, and his son. Before starting DairyCo, Mr Manh worked for a milk company located in northern Vietnam.

He was an astute engineer, able to take old machinery and extend its life well beyond its expected usefulness. That was an important skill, because the northern milk company never seemed to have enough budget to invest in the latest milk pasteurising and packaging equipment. But it did have access to an abundant supply of fresh milk from the agricultural region outside of Hanoi.

The northern milk company produced fresh milk and ultra-high-temperature (UHT) processed milk, which has a long shelf-life without the need for refrigeration – an important feature in Vietnam, where the cold supply chain was still in its infancy and erratic in its dependability. But realising the growth potential for fresh milk in the early 2000s, Mr Manh started DairyCo in 2004. He held an 80% stake in the new company while his friends owned the other 20%.

DairyCo's strategy was fairly simple: take advantage of cooperative farming in the northern part of Vietnam to produce fresh UHT and pasteurised milk, as well as yoghurt. Cooperative farming meant that the local farms would own and raise two to six cows per household. DairyCo would provide the calves, animal feed, and medicines in return for their milk. The cows would be milked twice a day, at 6am and 6pm, and the milk would be delivered to local collection points which happened to be owned by local government leaders.

The farmers would get paid by the litre and a DairyCo representative would always be on site at the time of milking to ensure that the milk was of the highest quality. This was to prevent the common problem of milk being diluted with water. In 2008, a major scandal occurred in China when it was discovered that some farmers were introducing melamine into water-diluted milk to ensure that it would pass the high-protein-content test. Although such an aberration never occurred in Vietnam, water dilution happened regularly.

DairyCo was able get an average of 15 to 18 litres of milk per cow per day, far lower than the average production of dairy cows in New Zealand or the US, but enough to make a profit for both the farmers and the company. When we started to evaluate investing in DairyCo in 2013, the company's cooperative farmers included 3,000 household farms and about 12,000 cows for milking.

In 2013, DairyCo had the production capacity of 120,000 tons of milk and yoghurt per year in its three production plants and generated an annual revenue of $50m. Profits reached around $2m. However, its balance sheet was weak, and the debt burden was much too high to be serviced by the current cash flow.

In 2009, DairyCo took on debt to invest in machinery and other equipment. This appeared sound at the time, but a trade deficit, a currency that was devaluing against the USD, and too much credit growth (30% to 50% per annum) in the years 2009–2011 meant that Vietnam experienced significant inflation in 2011. And as interest rates on loans typically reset every three to six months – there are no fixed-rate loans in Vietnam – all this meant that interest rates increased significantly, to over 20%. Suddenly, it became much more expensive for DairyCo to service its debt.

VinaCapital was invited in to help recapitalise DairyCo's balance sheet. Under the terms of the proposed agreement, we would invest $30m – $22.5m of which would be injected into the business and $7.5m was money out to the family – in exchange for 40% of the business and a commitment from the sponsor, Mr Manh and his management team to grow the business.

One of the major accounting firms was courting VinaCapital to invest in the business on the back of strong revenue growth potential (which was forecast 41% CAGR from 2012 to 2017), driven by:

1. Strong penetration into the northern Vietnam market;

2. Strong brand recognition in the north and south of Vietnam;

3. Substantial investment in marketing, including TV advertising campaigns;

4. Strong nationwide distribution network;

5. Fresh milk sourcing – 100% sourced from fresh milk in Vietnam; and

6. Management team – highly experienced and well connected.

At the time, 2013, we held a big stake in the leading milk company in Vietnam, Vinamilk, so we were quite familiar with the dynamics and growth of the market. Vietnam was consuming milk at an average of around 20 litres per person, while its neighbours, Thailand and Malaysia, were consuming about 30 to 60 litres per capita per annum. Obviously, there was a lot of upside in terms of demand and growth.

In 2012, the size of Vietnam's dairy market was valued at approximately $2.4bn, of which UHT milk and yoghurt comprised $1.1bn. And the market was expected to double by 2015, particularly in the UHT milk and yoghurt segments.

The growth prospects for the market looked very promising. DairyCo also had what we believed to be a key competitive advantage: the fact that it sourced its milk 100% fresh from Vietnamese farmers. In Vietnam, approximately 65% of drinking milk is produced by recombining fresh milk with milk powder, which is imported primarily from New Zealand.

Sold on the prospects for the market and the company, we began our due diligence and began negotiations. Eventually, we were comfortable enough with what we knew and were prepared to invest. However, before doing so, we asked a certain Mr Tuan to join DairyCo as CEO. Mr Tuan was well known to us and to the industry; he successfully led sales and marketing at a large F&B company and had also worked at a major multinational when it entered the Vietnamese market in the 1990s. He came on board, reporting to Mr Manh, and the two of them committed to growing the business as we requested based on our discussions with them.

The investment

In November 2014, more than a year and a half after that first meeting with Mr Manh on that sultry day in May, VinaCapital finally invested in DairyCo. But the terms were completely different from what the major accounting firm had originally envisioned a year earlier. The terms we agreed to were:

- $44.7m for a 70% stake, of which $19.7m was money out to the existing shareholder to acquire their shares and $25m went into the business.

- Valuation was $38.3m and $63.3m, pre-money and post-money respectively. This pre-money valuation is about 0.5× price to 2014 sales ratio, price-to-book ratio (P/B) of 3.4×

and enterprise value (EV)/EBITDA of 24×; this compared to Vinamilk's multiple P/S of 3.6×, P/B of 6.3× and EV/EBITDA of 12× at the time.

- At the time of VinaCapital's exit, if the business was valued at less than $125m but more than $100m, the sponsor was to transfer to VinaCapital an additional 10% based on a sliding scale from $125m to $100m. If the value was below $100m, the sponsor would not transfer anything more than the 10% already transferred.

- VinaCapital effectively controlled the business, with Mr Tuan as the CEO. Mr Manh relinquished the chairman's seat (although he remained a significant minority shareholder) and a VinaCapital executive took on that role.

Some of the assumptions around the performance of the business were:

- 2013 sales were $50m and sales for 2014 were expected to be $75.5m.

- 2014 expected EBITDA was $2.6m, and the business was expected to break even or record a slight loss.

- Total assets at 2014 year-end were $41m and total liabilities were $21m.

- Expected revenue for 2015 was to be around $110m, with EBITDA and net profit to be $5m and $1m respectively.

Investment year 1/2015: New products eclipse old ones

In the first full year that we were invested, 2015, the management team projected net sales of $110m and a profit before tax of almost $3m. In actuality, the sales result was

79% of the budget, at $86m, while profit before tax was barely above zero, at less than $300,000.

The team focused on launching a couple of new product lines and, as such, put a lot of marketing dollars behind them. Most of the marketing budget went toward producing and airing TV commercials. This focus on new products resulted in the older, more established products losing market share as growth deteriorated. While total net revenue came in far below expectation, it was still 34% higher than in 2014.

At that time, the global prices for powdered milk began to decline, while prices for fresh milk bought from Vietnamese farmers remain unchanged. Since the company was committed to buying fresh milk at certain prices from the local farmers, it was difficult for them to adjust the purchasing cost. As such, the company started experiencing a rapid decline in gross margin for products that included fresh milk.

Nevertheless, at the end of 2015, the balance sheet looked relatively strong, with current assets of almost $20m and liabilities of less than $10m. Inventory balance was at a reasonable level.

Investment year 2/2016: Sales force quits, milk powder prices drop

DairyCo management committed to sales of $120m and profit before tax of a little less than $3m. This was also a year of planned investment in new machinery and equipment, as well as increasing inventory to meet higher sales and take advantage of more processing capacity. At the end of 2016, the company budgeted to have cash of a little over $10m, while inventory doubled relative to 2015, and debt was expected to increase to over $20m – predominantly in accounts payable.

Actual performance for 2016 was terrible. Net revenue was $65m, or almost half of the planned amount, and the company recorded a loss of over $11m. Needless to say, investors were being asked to provide a shareholder's loan to continue operations.

Company management blamed competition for the poor results, as well as a lack of leadership on the sales team. DairyCo did not have a proper customer-resource-management system at the time of our investment. During 2016, the team began to migrate to a new system, which caused terrible headaches for the sales team and resulted in more than half of them leaving. On top of this, the cost of powdered milk continued to be half that of fresh-milk. This put DairyCo and other fresh milk producers at a significant disadvantage.

Investment year 3/2017: Losses accumulate, time to change leadership

In the third year of investment, 2017, management committed to delivering sales of $90m and a smaller loss of less than $4m, but also requested that shareholders inject another $20m into the company. We ended up providing a $10m convertible loan (which would convert into a 10.5% stake in the business) at an interest rate of 5% and acquiring another 10.5% of DairyCo through a new issuance for $10m.

At this stage, VinaCapital has invested $54.7m in equity and owned 82.1% of DairyCo, with a convertible bond of $10m that could take VinaCapital's stake up to 84% if converted. In total, $64.7m of value was at risk.

In the third quarter of 2017, it became clear that sales would fall far short of the promised $90m. The run rate was pointing at a total net revenue of slightly over $60m, even worse than in 2016. On top of that, a $10m loss was projected.

After a couple years of broken commitments, it was time to make changes at the top. We recruited a new COO to handle day-to-day leadership and repositioned the CEO, Mr Tuan, as the chairman. The year closed with sales of $56m and a loss of $11.7m. And lo and behold, the management team asked VinaCapital for another shareholder loan of $8m.

Investment year 4/2018: A turnaround begins to take shape

In the fourth year of our investment, 2018, management promised total net sales to be $77m and loss to be around $2.5m. By this point, we had little confidence in their ability to perform. However, during the year we seconded a senior executive from VinaCapital into DairyCo to effectively run the business side-by-side with the new COO.

In July 2018, performance started to pivot to a positive EBITDA, a sight not seen for a long time. For the remainder of the year, DairyCo delivered positive EBITDA each month, and at year-end, revenue totalled $55m while the loss was 'just' $600,000. All things considered, not a horrible result.

What changed in 2018?

The new leadership undertook a major restructuring of operations and drastically cut spending on marketing and advertising. As part of the restructuring, the team took a hard look at inventory management, sales, and distribution, and what they found was troubling. Inventory was stagnant in the distribution system, and the sales team was pushing too much product on to retailers when there was not enough demand.

That meant that unsold cartons of milk or containers of yoghurt sat on shelves for a while, and as they neared their expiration dates, their prices had to be constantly discounted in order to move them. When such discounts occur regularly, it is impossible to push new products at the manufacturer's suggested retail price. The team slowed the push and introduced products that were more acceptable to the market. Additionally, the commission programme for the sales team was restructured to focus on products being pulled through retail channels, rather than pushed.

Even the placement of the product on store shelves was incorrect. Higher fees were paid to put DairyCo products at eye-level – usually a good spot if a product is targeted toward adults. But many products were aimed at children and featured cartoon characters on the packaging – they couldn't see those products. That was corrected. Finally, this issue also revealed that senior leadership did not venture out into the field to see where and how products were sold with their own eyes – they were detached from parts of the business.

DairyCo was able to flush through fresh milk that was still priced at a slightly higher level than powdered milk. In terms of marketing, the company did not go 'dark'. Rather, it moved away from expensive television commercials and utilised social media in conjunction with influencers, events and promotions. These and other actions significantly contributed to the company's much smaller loss for the year.

Investment year 5/2019: The stage is set for a sale

In the fifth year of our investment, the VinaCapital executive took over as the permanent CEO. Our executive and the DairyCo team committed to sales and EBITDA of $60 and

$1m respectively. Thanks to further restructuring steps, DairyCo delivered actual revenue of $82m, almost 40% higher than planned, while EBITDA came in at almost $9m, significantly higher than planned. Profit before tax totalled nearly $5m.

We thought the company was in a position where a sale was feasible, so we began to target strategic buyers onshore in Vietnam as well as offshore.

Over the course of the year, we engaged in negotiations with a large Asian multinational. Although discussions looked promising at one point, it became clear that the challenges of acquiring and operating the business in Vietnam, where it had a limited presence, were probably more than it wished to handle.

Investment year 6/2020: A local strategic buyer seizes the opportunity

In early 2020, we were approached by the owner of a well-known milk company based in southern Vietnam, who we will call Mr Quy. This company produces fresh, carton milk that effectively lasts ten days. This is different from pasteurised milk packaged in a UHT container, which can last six months or more at room temperature. Mr Quy had been trying to exit his controlling stake in the southern fresh-milk purveyor, but since it was so small, he had a difficult time convincing a strategic buyer to acquire it at the valuation he was seeking.

Rather than selling his company at a lower-than-desired valuation, Mr Quy saw in DairyCo an opportunity to create a larger company by acquiring another player that complemented his own. There were clear synergies between the companies, and DairyCo had an extensive distribution network, particularly in the north, and a good range of products in its portfolio. He contacted us about acquiring our 80% stake and after a few months of back and forth amid Covid-19, we reached an agreement.

We were able to come to terms quickly because Mr Quy was a savvy domestic financier, and as a result, the hurdles that a foreign buyer might have encountered were not an issue. In July 2020, VinaCapital announced that it had completed the partial divestment of its stake in DairyCo, generating an IRR on our investment of 1.5×. The following month, we announced that we had completed our divestment.

In 2021, DairyCo continues to grow with strength. The pandemic has led domestic consumers to buy more groceries through the modern trade (as opposed to the wet market) and online channels, significantly increasing demand for DairyCo products.

Additionally, DairyCo was able to capitalise on the difficulties some of the competing international brands encountered during the period of restricted movement in April and May 2020. Some of those companies experienced a breakdown in logistics which caused a lack of inventory in the modern trade, and DairyCo was able to win over some of their customers.

Vietnamese people now consume about 27 litres of dairy per year, according to the Vietnam Industry Research and Consultancy, while consumption is projected to rise by 7% in 2021.[19] This suggests that there continues to be room for growth for companies that can evolve with the changing needs (and appetites) of the Vietnamese consumer.

---

19 "How will the dairy industry fare in 2021?", *VnExpress*, 18 January 2021.

Lessons learned

DairyCo was one of our most challenging investments in recent years, and it underscored the importance of several of the 20 rules. In particular:

- **Trust in management is key.** We trusted the existing management to execute against the commitments they made with us, but they repeatedly failed to perform – they lost our trust. The CEO we brought in when we invested was very accomplished in a particular area but didn't have the full portfolio of expertise we wanted to see, which ultimately contributed to him failing to meet commitments.

- **Don't take a controlling stake.** We are financial investors – operating companies is not what we do. Ultimately, one of my team members stepped up to fill the CEO role, requiring this individual's full attention, and was able to turn things around. Fortunately, things worked out for the best. But it was tough going for many years, with an outcome that was not at all guaranteed.

- **No money out.** When we first invested, $20m immediately went out to buy out the shareholders, Mr Manh and some of the others – they cashed out. As a result, Mr Manh had little skin left in the game, and while he initially remained chairman, his interest in the company waned. In fact, he used some of the proceeds to start a new company that made milk pudding desserts. His son, however, remained a shareholder until we sold our stake in 2020.

- **Alignment of interests.** Again, Mr Manh's interests were not aligned with ours after he cashed out. Management were not shareholders and did not feel sufficiently incentivised to perform. We immediately worked to better align interests by implementing an ESOP, even though it slightly diluted our stake.

CONCLUSION

There is no market for investing more exciting than Vietnam is today. If there was, I wouldn't stay here. This is a country that has roared back to life after decades of conflict. It ticks all of the boxes: a large population that is educated and still reasonably young; a growing middle class that is eager to spend; and a stable government that is committed to ongoing economic reforms that will improve the lives of its citizens.

Vietnam is probably the last country that is likely to follow the East Asian model of development that countries like South Korea, Taiwan, and ultimately, China, were able to effectively apply and become the successes they are today. They all made the progression from poor, largely agrarian nations to urbanised manufacturing powerhouses, with high (or increasing) standards of living.

Foreign investment is playing an important role in Vietnam's growth. Whether it is huge multinationals like Samsung building factories and research-and-development facilities and employing thousands of people, or investment firms like VinaCapital, which are helping home-grown small and mid-sized businesses expand and realise their potential, international investment in Vietnam will continue to be essential for the foreseeable future. The potential for great profit continues to be enormous.

But if one thing should be clear after reading this book, it's that investing in Vietnam can be tricky. It carries all the risks of frontier and emerging markets and will continue to do so for a while. Experienced international institutional and retail investors alike need to be aware of those risks and plan for them accordingly.

Investing in listed stocks is probably the safest bet for investors who want to participate in Vietnam's markets. There are some very good, well-managed companies now listed on Vietnam's stock exchange, and liquidity and disclosure are improving every year. Sooner or later, the country will graduate to emerging market status too, which should prompt enormous inflows into the market.

While more challenging, it is private-equity investing that continues to excite me and my team. After all, we are playing a contributory role in helping an entrepreneur build his or her company into something bigger. The three key principles we must always remember are:

1. Ensure your interests are aligned with those of management.

2. Document as much as possible and do thorough due diligence.

3. Have an exit strategy right from the beginning and stay focused on it.

If you keep these core principle at the front of your mind, the likelihood of an investment going completely off the rails is minimised. Private-equity investing is immensely satisfying, from both a personal and professional standpoint. And it usually generates strong returns for investors along the way.

Vietnam is in a very unique position at the moment, registering solid economic growth despite a global pandemic, continuing to increase its engagement with the world as some other countries turn inward, and positioning itself for much more to come. The risks remain, but so do considerable rewards for those who are aware of the risks, know how to plan for and mitigate them, and have a medium- to long-term outlook – this is not a market in which to make a quick buck.

I always encourage investors to learn more about this vibrant country before the secret is totally out. Follow the 20 rules I have laid out in this book, and the chance that you'll successfully cross the street that is investing in Vietnam is high.

ACKNOWLEDGEMENTS

The invitation to gather my Vietnam investment experiences and put them down on paper gave me a rare chance to reflect on the excitement of my journey thus far. More importantly, it gives me a chance to recognise a few of the people who have helped me succeed along the way.

Having a comfortable life in Austin, Texas, working for Dell, one of the largest technology companies in the world, and getting to invest money from its balance sheet was a dream that most can never imagine. However, that was not to be the long path. I want to thank my wife, Tina Nguyen, who is probably the smartest person in my life, for encouraging me to take the road less travelled and move back to Vietnam.

Our migration from the US to Vietnam with our two-year-old son was a path in the opposite direction of most immigrants, including myself, once a boat person. This move entailed many major changes in our lives. So not only am I thankful for my wife's encouragement, but also for her leadership in getting us through these major changes. Leading the family isn't the only thing she is good at – she runs one of the world's largest multinational life-insurance companies' business in Vietnam and ranks as one of their few female CEOs.

My investment journey in Vietnam started out at Prudential Vietnam (now called Eastspring Investments) which was led by Alex Hambly. It was there, at one of the most conservative investment shops, that I learned about the challenges and rewards that come with investing in Vietnam. We got first-hand experience in seeing what could go wrong over the course of our investment in the largest domestic-animal-feed business. A lack of ethics and governance issues led us down a path of holding the check book for one year, which ultimately allowed us to recover from our mistakes, but more importantly, take lessons from them.

But it was at VinaCapital where I gained most of the experience documented in this book, and where I continue to learn and invest to this day. I want to thank my partners, Don Lam, the company's co-founder and CEO, and Brook Taylor, the COO, for their encouragement, support, and leadership.

Don invited me to join VinaCapital in late 2006. It took a while to iron out the details, but over the course of our negotiations it became clear to me that there are three key attributes that a person requires to become a truly successful investment manager. First, they must be able to manage customers and investors, for example, being able to raise money and keep investors happy; second, manage their greatest asset – their people; and third, consistently deliver profits and returns on investments.

VinaCapital afforded me the opportunity to hone my skills in all three areas, while Dell and Prudential, investing what we call captive money, did not allow me to experience the world, stress, and travel of fundraising. To this day, I encourage all my senior team members to learn how to excel in each of these three critical areas.

I am fortunate that I have the greatest asset an investment manager could ask for, the investment professionals who make up my team. I have been fortunate to have had really smart people leading and supporting some of our more successful investments, including Ms Nguyen Thi Dieu Phuong and Ms Dang Pham Minh Loan. Men like me were really only there to lend support. As I have stated, I truly believe that women make great investment professionals and business leaders. Some of the most successful businesses in Vietnam are run by women, a subject I may write about in my next book.

Finally, this book is the result of the work and support of a few people. It was very stop and start, and it took a while for things to get going, but I want to thank Joel Weiden for ultimately writing this book with me and getting it over the line. Khanh Vu, from my team, also helped refresh my memory and fill in some details.

There are many others I would like to thank and acknowledge, and I sincerely apologise that I cannot include them all here. I will be sure to acknowledge you in the next book!

Andy Ho

December 31, 2020